Carol,
    Thank you for
spirit to Paloman Herim Laboratories &
And, please accept this egotistic gift.
I feel the need to share with you
who I am.

                     Jerry Kolins, MD
                     Medical Director
                     Paloma Health Laboratories

Life Is What Happens While You Make Other Plans

Life Is What Happens While You Make Other Plans

A MEMOIR

Jerry Kolins

Ann Arbor, MI

Published in the United States of America by
Michigan Publishing
Manufactured in the United States of America

DOI: http://doi.org/10.3998/mpub.12250217

ISBN 978-1-60785-709-9 (hardcover)
ISBN 978-1-60785-710-5 (ebook)
ISBN 978-1-60785-711-2 (open access)

An imprint of Michigan Publishing, Maize Books serves the publishing needs
of the University of Michigan community by making high-quality scholarship
widely available in print and online. It represents a new model for authors
seeking to share their work within and beyond the academy, offering
streamlined selection, production, and distribution processes. Maize Books
is intended as a complement to more formal modes of publication in a wide
range of disciplinary areas.
http://www.maizebooks.org

Cover photo by Jerry Kolins, taken in Wailea, Maui, in February 2021

This book is dedicated to my wife of over forty years. Dale possesses the two secret ingredients that account for longevity in marriage: tolerance and adaptability. I was not blessed with either trait.

Contents

Introduction

I am fascinated by human behavior and the scope of our ability to reason. I consider myself a scientist, but for me, it is the creative and performing arts that define humanity.

All scientific accomplishments are destined to be recognized—usually by several investigators at the same time. Even Charles Darwin's theory of natural selection was codiscovered with Alfred Russel Wallace. Did you know that?

Scientific discovery is inevitable, but human behavior and our ability to reason evolve. What captivates our imagination today? What haunts us throughout our lives? What makes us laugh and what makes us cry? I wrote these short essays to reveal just that.

Some of these essays may bring back special memories to the reader; others may cause you to pray for a selective dose of Alzheimer's disease. In either case, these events help me define humanity.

And about those events in your life that you wish would evaporate from your consciousness, consider the possibility that whatever embarrassment or disappointment you may have caused yourself, everyone else has long since forgotten it.

ONE

The Early Years

Pineapple Upside-Down Cake

I wonder how old most of us are when we first think to wish our parents a happy anniversary. I was about fourteen years old when it occurred to me that getting Mom and Dad an anniversary gift would be a beautiful thing to do. My parents were married on May 12, 1945. It was circa 1961 when I got the idea all on my own. Perhaps you would call me a late bloomer. So I described my plan to my brother, Mark, who was ten, and my sister, Joan, who was four.

My plan was to get an anniversary cake and have it double as an anniversary gift. Of course, we all enjoyed our own birthdays. And we expected some gift from Mom and Dad (the cake didn't count). I guess I am confessing a certain amount of spoilage, though deep inside, I think we were raised with the proper balance of love and discipline. When you are living on an allowance, this approach seems cost-conscious. Many have since told me that the cake may have been the last cost-conscious decision of my life.

In 1961, May 12 was a Friday. That was perfect. We would buy the cake after school on Friday and hide it under my bed until that night. We would light the sixteen candles on the cake, and the three of us would sing "Happy Anniversary to You."

It was just not to be.

When I got to the bakery, there were too many choices. What kind of cake do adults like? Kids like chocolate, a lot of whipped cream, and icing. But this just didn't seem right for an adult. I asked the woman behind the counter what type of cake she would recommend for an anniversary and eventually settled on one with slices of pineapple on top and between the layers. The bakery worker removed the cake from the display counter and assembled a cardboard box so I could carry the cake home. I remember this long string that hung from the ceiling above the counter. In what seemed like one circular motion, the woman waiting on me wrapped the string around the box, securing all six sides. I took the cake home.

My brother and sister and I were learning the joy of giving. Until then, we had only understood the joy of receiving. The box was placed under my bed until all three of us agreed it was time to activate the plan. We waited until after dinner.

In the bedroom, we pulled out the cake and placed the sixteen candles on top. Back in 1961, smoking was common, and there were plenty of matchbooks around the house. We lit all the candles, and I picked up the cake for a surprise delivery.

We lived in a townhouse in Queens, New York, with three bedrooms and the only bathroom in the house on the second floor. The first floor had a living room, dining room, and kitchen. We also had a basement. Firmly holding the blazing pastry, I stepped out of the bedroom followed by my brother, then my sister. We tiptoed down the stairs.

I can still remember the excitement I felt at that moment. It was almost like Christmas morning—only this time, the gifts were not for us. The three of us would surely be remembered as loving children. And the truth be known, that was the purpose of the plan. Kids can be demanding. We were mature enough to realize our parents needed to know we appreciated all they did for us.

We decided we would start singing "Happy Anniversary to You" when we were halfway down the stairs. We did. My parents came into the living room from the kitchen to enjoy what was truly a surprise. We got that part right, but the rest was not part of the choreography.

The scene can only be viewed as if in slow motion. I guess I needed more practice in the art of tiptoeing. My right foot missed a step just a few feet from the landing. Over I went. The cake sailed

Mom in the 1940s.

through the air. It was free-falling. Briefly, I wondered if I could catch this thing before it hit the carpet. Then I realized it had no hope of landing candles up. The bright lights were extinguished in one thud as the top of the cake hit the floor.

My memory is a little foggy on what happened next. I feel sure my eyes filled with tears. Mark could not comprehend how his big brother could be so clumsy and ruin the surprise. He may have expressed his disappointment rather explicitly. I don't remember my sister's reaction. But I distinctly remember my mother running over to the scene of the crime and proclaiming, "That is the most beautiful pineapple upside-down cake I've ever seen!"

Of course, this was no consolation to a fourteen-year-old. It took a while before I realized Mom was saying "I love you too."

The Sobbing Sofa, or How I Became the "Obedient One"

The sobbing sofa conjures up visions of a common room in Harry Potter in which the sofa actually cries. Here's a story about a sobbing sofa in which only the adolescents who sit on it sob.

Growing up in the borough of Queens, New York City, I lived on a block that had attached houses from one end of the street to the other. Except for the houses on the corner, each house shared lateral walls with its neighbors on each side. In our house, when you walked through the front door, there was a minifoyer with a closet. Take one step to the right, and you were in the living room—the location of the sofa.

The width of the front half of the house on the first floor was all living room. The living room extended to a partition that demarcated the dining room from the living area. The kitchen was next to the dining room. I'd estimate the length of the house at about fifty feet.

There was a window at each end of the house. The living room window overlooked Seventy-Seventh Road. The dining room window overlooked the backyard. Upstairs were the three bedrooms. Downstairs was the basement, a concept common on the East Coast. The sofa was up against the living room window, facing the interior, so one could look through the dining room and see the window on the opposite side of the house. When Mom walked out of the kitchen and looked to the right, she could see all the activity going on in the living room. The sofa was straight ahead, and just out of sight on the right was a Sylvania TV.

I am the oldest, so I was the first to study algebra. My brother, Mark, was probably watching TV. My sister was three years old when I sat on the sofa with Dad for "homework review."

The author at age six.

This concept of "homework review" with Dad started when I was in the third grade. I had established a pattern of incomplete homework assignments, believing that such tasks were to be completed at the discretion of the student. Dad thought homework was compulsory. Mom supported Dad. It was now 1960, I was thirteen years old, and Dad was teaching me algebra.

Algebra was taught on the sobbing sofa. I remember initially thinking that algebra was fun. After a short while, I suggested to Dad that we no longer needed to continue homework review because my new trend was one of responsibility. I did the homework and liked it. Dad disagreed. He said I wouldn't know if I had made a mistake unless he reviewed it. I was a little pissed, but I reasoned that I wouldn't make a mistake. That would show him.

But I did make a mistake. He called me from the TV to the sofa for my evening education. As I recall, the problem was something like this: Four years ago, Jerry's age was half the age he will be in ten years. How old is Jerry today? Dad was strict about the approach to the solution. I was to take an 8½″ × 11″ piece of paper and fold it in half, and half again, thus dividing the sheet of paper into four quadrants.

Right off the bat, I challenged Dad. Why did we need to fold the paper? You could get the correct answer whether the paper was folded or not. He said we had eight problems to review. Each quadrant on either side of the paper would be used for one of the eight problems. I insisted we could do this without folding the paper. The area on a sheet of paper wouldn't change by folding it. He decided to teach me a lesson. If I got all eight problems on this sheet of paper, I could decide whether the paper should be folded in the future. If I couldn't get all eight problems on this single sheet of paper, then we would do it Dad's way in the future. Deal.

I couldn't do it. I didn't understand that psychologically, seeing all the space on a page caused me to write larger than I would if you gave me only 25 percent of the space. We did it Dad's way from then on.

About the solution to the above problem: There was only one approach—Dad's approach. First, you must write,

Let x = Jerry's age now

Four years ago, Jerry was (x − 4)

When Jerry was (x − 4), he was ½(x + 10)

$$x - 4 = (x + 10) / 2$$

The next step is to multiply each side by 2 and get

$$2x - 8 = x + 10$$

$$x = 18$$

Here is where it got contentious. Look at the line that reads $x - 4 = (x + 10) / 2$. The temptation was too great. I did not follow Dad's direction. I completed the arithmetic in my head and shouted out "X equals eighteen!" Dad said I was wrong because you don't get credit for getting the right answer if you don't show the correct work. I was so frustrated that tears welled up in my eyes. This is how an ordinary living room couch got the name "sobbing sofa." The sofa maintained that distinction when it was Mark's turn and then Joan's. But we all scored a perfect 100 percent on the algebra Regents standardized examination given to all ninth graders in New York State.

This also explains why I became the "obedient one."

The front door of my childhood home in Queens. Walk through the door, and on the right, you would soon confront the sobbing sofa, which was placed in front of those two windows.

Wel-Met Camps and the
Naïveté of Adolescence, Part 1

I was a camper and eventually a counselor at Wel-Met. My first year was the summer after eighth grade. That was in 1960. I remember my bunk was no. 72.

Let me introduce Wel-Met via an article published in the *New York Times* on April 24, 2005, by Michael Pollak:

> Wel-Met survives in memory and online, thanks to thousands of nostalgic alumni. Wel-Met, which had divisions in Narrowsburg, Barryville, and Silver Lake in Sullivan County, was founded as the Metropolitan Jewish Centers Camp Association in May 1935 and became one of the nation's largest sleep-away camps, with well over 1,000 campers a summer. According to some ex-campers, the name stood for Welfare Metropolitan. Like many other low-cost camps run by nonprofit associations, it fell victim to rising expenses, declining government aid, and a change in trends from no-frills to more luxurious and specialty camps. Many alumni—Howard Stern was a camper—correspond enthusiastically about memories of forests and lakes and dining-hall bug juice on a Web site at www.wel-metcamps.com/.*

When I got to Narrowsburg in 1960, I was excited about being at a "sleep-away" camp. There were two sessions, a six-week session and a three-week session. I pleaded to be sent for six weeks and got my wish. Our bunks were described as "lean-tos." That's a wooden cabin with a lean-to roof open on one end. We called the open side the "front" of the cabin. If you liked camping in a tent or in a lean-to, if you liked hiking, playing softball, and swimming, you loved this rustic camp.

Wel-Met wasn't so far into the woods that you couldn't have pizza; it just wasn't the kind of pizza most New York City kids were used to. I had my first pizza in the third or fourth grade. I

---

* Michael Pollak, "Wel-Met Memories," *New York Times*, April 24, 2005.

My parents circa 1950. Dad taught me algebra, and Mom focused on
teaching me about poetry and the arts.

was watching *Your Hit Parade* with Gisele MacKenzie when Mom
and Dad walked in the door carrying a big box. The first pizza,
from Enzio's, was just tomato and mozzarella but tasted out of this
world. My brother, Mark, spent last year trying to duplicate Enzio's
achievement, and he finally succeeded. I tested it and confirmed
the original aroma and taste. Today I still judge all pizzas against the
gold standard, Enzio's, which was on Main Street in Flushing circa

1955. Today, you can use my brother's accomplishment as the new gold standard.

Well, who would have guessed we were going to have pizza at rustic Wel-Met? I started to get suspicious when my counselor announced to the entire bunk that we would be making our own. This way we would learn how it is done. Really?

Even more amazing to a group of thirteen-year-olds was that we would make the pizza during a camping trip. We would stuff our backpacks with our paraphernalia, leave our bunks, carry a tent, pitch the tent, make a campfire, and cook pizza!

The pizza wouldn't match Enzio's, but we would dine under the stars around a campfire. That's an A+ for ambience.

We all gathered around the campfire for our pizza lesson. We were handed a piece of white bread. Then the counselor, Dick Wernick, showed us how to pierce the bread with the sticks we thought were for marshmallows. We were then handed a packet of ketchup and a slice of American cheese. Campers were directed to put that cheese on the white bread, add the ketchup, and toast over the campfire. Voilà—pizza a la Wel-Met.

I still loved the experience.

Wel-Met Camps was a rustic haven for New York City kids.

Wel-Met Camps, Part 2

Even though Wel-Met Camps no longer exists, there must have been something special about that experience because there is a very active website, www.wel-metcamps.com, where past campers and counselors share memories, photos, and experiences.

I was part of the Pioneer Unit in Narrowsburg, New York, in 1961, and I considered that summer to be preparation for the Western Trip, which would be in 1962. The Western Trip marked the last experience for a Wel-Met camper due to the maximum age requirement. In 1963, I was hired as a "boat boy" in Barryville, New York. Yes, I was hired by Wel-Met and received my first W-2 form.

The Pioneer Unit consisted of about six to ten tents that were pitched on raised wooden floors and, as I remember, secured with bolts and turnbuckles. We didn't pitch these tents. We just spent six weeks learning how to live in them. Pitching tents in the dark and in the rain would come the next year.

My memories of Wel-Met include experiences at camp and experiences off-site, including reunions. Coney Island was a favorite reunion site. First, I'll share an on-site Wel-Met story.

Bruce Sankin was one of my bunkmates in Pioneers. He told jokes, and he did it well. He was an extrovert type that I imagine would be superb in marketing and sales. One night in 1961, he told a joke that I remember to this day. We were fifteen and sixteen years old, and some kids' jokes were X-rated—but not Bruce's. It went like this: One day a man walks into a grocery store and says, "Sir, may I have one pound of kidley beans?" The grocer says, "What did you say?" The man repeats himself and says, "One pound of kidley beans, please." The grocer says, "We don't have kidley beans, but we do have kidney beans." The man says to the grocer, "I said kidney, didel I?"

And here is another story, from Artie, who believed rules were meant to be broken. Because I was obedient, Artie was a fascination to me.

One day, Artie heard another camper say, "I wish we could have candy for our afternoon snack instead of Graham crackers." Artie

Mom with my sister, Joan, at Wel-Met Camps.

asked, "Like what?" The bunk shot back a list of popular candies like M&M's, Hershey bars, Chunky bars (remember Arnold Stang saying "Chunky, what a chunk of chocolate!"), and Oreo cookies. Artie replied, "OK, give me the money, and I will go to town and buy the candy." Many campers handed him money. But no camper was permitted off the campgrounds. That was the rule. It didn't apply to Artie.

After sunset, Artie walked out of Narrowsburg to the neighboring town of Silver Lake. When I awoke the next morning, I saw that Artie had emptied a shopping bag of goodies on the floor of the tent. Every single request was met. He was insubordinate and got away with it.

But my favorite Artie story occurred at a Coney Island reunion. We were enjoying the rides. They had something like the Disneyland Autopia—little gasoline-powered cars we could drive. Artie was in front of me and kept hitting the side wall of the track. I thought he really needed driving lessons. His antics were bashing up the car. But then the impossible happened: He drove the car at just the right angle so that it leaped the high curb, and he escaped. He drove away while one of the guys attending to the ride chased him down the street. I often wonder if Artie evaded jail time.

My sister, Joan, and brother, Mark, stand in front of me in this picture, taken on our way to the Wel-Met summer camps in upstate New York.

My personal memory of Coney Island was a warning I received from Bruce Sankin. He told me to put all my money in my sock except for a few dollars in my wallet. I asked why. He said that I should just do it. Before we left Coney Island, a rather nasty-appearing man came at me and said, "Give me your wallet." I hesitated, looked up at the thief, and realized I should cooperate. I opened my wallet, gave him the few dollars in it, and he left. I was safe. And I had 90 percent of my money in my sock. It's a jungle out there.

Junior High School

My First Love

F irst *love* causes many of us to think of an adolescent experiencing that early fascination with someone of the opposite sex. That definition worked in 1959. She was Roberta. I was twelve and in the eighth grade.

Parsons Junior High School (P.S. 168) in the borough of Queens, New York City, had a rectangular concrete playground adjacent to the school. I saw her there for the first time. She was athletic with a bouncy ponytail of long red hair and had no freckles. The hair caught my eye first. She was hard to miss. Playing in the schoolyard was fun. I was a bit too young to feel more than fun. But that changed the next year.

Dating in ninth grade in NYC was not expensive for a kid with an allowance of a dollar, but I still had to watch my spending. That year, I took Roberta on our first date. My favorite way to spend a Saturday was a boat ride in New York Harbor, sailing by the Statue of Liberty. Note I say *sailing by*, not *sailing to* the Statue of Liberty. Let me explain.

In 1960, the Q25/34 bus brought us to the NYC subway for fifteen cents. We took the subway to Battery Park in downtown Manhattan, which was another fifteen cents. Finally, in Battery Park, we took the Staten Island Ferry for five cents. Total round trip in 1960 cost seventy cents to sail past the Statue of Liberty.

I am pretty sure that if you didn't get *off* the ferry at Staten Island, you didn't need to pay another nickel to get back to Manhattan. But we got off the ferry and walked around. I was a spendthrift even then.

In the ninth grade, I delivered groceries, which earned me enough to take Roberta out to other places, including the movies. What better place to go? Looking back now, I realize that movies provided me with many of life's important lessons, and they helped uncover hidden thoughts and emotions. Sometimes one line is worth a thousand words, so I have paid homage to films throughout this book with bits of movie dialogue you may well remember.

But in 1960, I was less concerned with cosmic truths and more concerned with Roberta. We held hands and dated during our first year at Jamaica High School. I was in love. Then came the devastation.

Roberta was having a birthday party. It may have been a sweet sixteen party. I found out about it when I asked a friend to join me bowling on a Saturday, but he said he couldn't because he was going to Roberta's party. I didn't know about it because I hadn't been invited. For an infatuated teenager, that was painful. I can still feel it in my chest when I think about hearing the news.

As weeks passed, Roberta avoided me. I tried to reunite us but to no avail. I wondered what I could have done to hurt her. That wonder didn't leave me until 2018.

David Hodes was my closest friend in high school. He knew all about me and Roberta. David still lives in NYC. I am in California. In 2018, we agreed to a reunion in NYC. We hadn't seen each other since 1984.

We met at the Ritz-Carlton on Central Park South and had dinner at the bar in the lobby. After reminiscing about teachers, classes, and the prom, I confessed to David that I was still tormented by my experience with Roberta. What could have happened that caused her to ostracize me so?

David had that look on his face that I remembered from high school. It was the look when the teacher asked a question and David knew the answer. "She didn't want to hurt you," he said. "Didn't you know that Roberta was gay?"

All I could say was, "You mean it wasn't my fault? I didn't do anything wrong?"

Now I understand what "I have need for closure" means. I felt a huge sense of relief. All these decades, I thought there was something wrong with me. Hearing this news made me feel I was OK. After all these years, I still needed that.

The Answers Are in the Back of the Book

In the eighth grade, my dad asked me if I wanted to learn algebra, a subject that normally was taught in ninth grade. I got excited by his offer for two reasons: First, algebra sounded so important. The word conjured up visions of real mathematicians. Algebra wasn't arithmetic. Second, I would be ahead of the ninth-grade class next September. "Let's do it," I said.

The world has changed. Today, algebra is probably taught in third grade. But to me, this was an exciting eighth-grade experience. I got the syllabus from the New York State Board of Regents, and we worked almost every weekday. Dad would always check my work, no matter how confident I was about my progress.

The textbook we used had answers in the back of the book, so I would check the answers before I handed my paper to Dad. But there was a catch. Only the odd-numbered problems were linked to answers. Even-numbered problems caused me some anxiety because I wouldn't know if I got them right until Dad said so.

Let's fast-forward to 1998 and CEDU, a school whose name is a form of a pseudoacronym thought by many to refer to the method by which children learn—that is, they "see" (CE) and then they "do" (DU). CEDU is the school our daughter, Jessica, attended after we learned of her substance abuse. The school had classes for the parents. The director, Mel Wasserman, knew the parents needed help as much as the students. There really is no evidence that Mel's approach to rehabilitation was effective. But parents like me needed hope. Mel provided that.

He once gave a lecture explaining the levels of knowledge. At the base of his pyramid was mysticism. I think of mysticism as more ethereal than the next level in his pyramid, belief. Above belief was thinking. At the top was feeling. A lot of what Mel taught was based on mysticism, not knowledge. It was tough to accept that feeling was the highest level of knowledge. It seemed that thinking earned that distinction.

I did not protest Mel's teachings because other parents in the class challenged this doctrine for me. But Mel would not yield. He insisted that we remember his teachings because one day, they would all make sense.

At the end of eighth grade, I had completed the algebra class, and I asked Dad for a final examination. He circled a few questions from each chapter and said, "Here you go." Most of the questions were odd-numbered. I remember starting to check for answers in the back of the book, but about halfway through, I stopped. I felt something I can only describe as assuredness. Everything felt certain, secure, and even guaranteed. I did not have to check anymore. I just knew all the answers were correct.

Thinking back on that experience, I concluded that Mel was right. Feeling was the highest level of knowledge. Yet every once in a while, when I am faced with one of life's dilemmas, I wish it were odd-numbered.

THREE

Senior High School

Ronnie

I t was early in the 1960s. The Beatles had not arrived yet, but we'd been enjoying Dion and the Belmonts ("Lonely Teenager"), Johnny Maestro & the Crests ("Step by Step"), and the Five Satins ("In the Still of the Night") long after these records had been released. They seemed to pair with the raging hormones of the teen years as well as La Tâche pairs with roast duck in my septuagenarian years.

Then there was folk music—that is, Joan Baez, Bob Dylan, Pete Seeger, Peter, Paul and Mary. Without these performers, the hormones were in constant control. These artists did the impossible. They got teenagers to think.

As for me, I was thinking about Ronnie. It was my junior year at Jamaica High School in Queens. At the age of fifteen, I considered Ronnie the most curvaceous member of the class of 1964. I had many thoughts about being alone with her. All these thoughts were X-rated.

David Hodes was my closest friend in high school, maybe my only friend, so I confided in him. I told him I wanted to date Ronnie. He said not to. I asked why. David told me he had taken Ronnie on a date, and from that single experience, he knew I should not date her.

The raging hormones accounted for my decision to ignore David's advice and ask her to the movies. She said yes. It certainly felt like this was the right decision. I do not remember the movie, but I will never forget that night.

After the movie, Ronnie politely invited me into her house and brought me to the basement. The basement was what people referred to then as a rec room. We sat down on a comfortable couch. Ronnie moved closer to me. I asked where her parents were. As she put her hand on my thigh, Ronnie said they were out of town and would return the next day.

I was fifteen, so I had unrealistic fears. Maybe one ejaculation could impregnate a room full of teenage girls. Birth control pills were invented in 1956, but they were not known to many students at Jamaica High in 1962–63. And if you asked me if I knew about oral contraceptives, I would have said I had heard about them, but I had no idea how reliable they were. I had to be careful. And Ronnie did not have an ounce of caution in her. She was full speed ahead, and it didn't take too long before I realized a decision had to be made. I decided on virginity and ran home where it was safe. I would not participate in any act that could result in me telling my father that I was going to be a father.

David knew me well, and his advice was sound, but I had to learn this lesson from experience. As a senior citizen, I occasionally think

Jamaica High School, which had the aura of Rydell High from the movie *Grease.*

about that night on the couch. Was it a missed opportunity? I don't suspect Ronnie ever thinks about it. But even to this day, I would like to tell her that it took only another three years to figure out how to do it. And I have been practicing ever since.

When Are You Supposed to Have Sex?

Growing up in New York City was dazzling, though I realized at the age of about seventeen that a smaller town and a slower pace might be better for me. In my early teens, I often took the bus on Parsons Boulevard to the subway station. Then it was the E train from Jamaica, Queens, to Manhattan. The train went under the East River, but I was too young to understand how that tunnel was built and always worried about the safety of that early twentieth-century construction.* I was relieved when we arrived at the first station in Manhattan, Lexington Avenue and Fifty-Third Street.

On one such trip, I was walking by the Metropole Cafe on Seventh Avenue and Forty-Eighth Street when two girls approached me. One of them asked if I was interested in a good time. Her eyes and hands moved in a manner that invited me to explore her attributes. I must admit, as a high school senior, I struggled to imagine anything more inviting.

For me, sex was like the moth and the flame story. I recall believing that if I accepted her offer at any price, it would be the best experience of my life. But the consequence would probably be syphilis or gonorrhea. In the 1960s, there were four reasons not to have sex:

---

* The tunnel technology was so innovative that in 1907, the Pennsylvania Railroad shipped a twenty-three-foot-diameter section of the new East River Tunnels to the Jamestown Exposition in Norfolk, Virginia, to celebrate the three hundredth anniversary of the nearby founding of the colony at Jamestown. The same tube, with an inscription indicating that it had been displayed at the exposition, was later installed underwater and remains in use. Construction was completed on the East River tunnels on March 18, 1908 (Wikipedia report based on information from *Industrial Magazine* in 1907 and the *New York Times* on March 19, 1908).

(1) syphilis, (2) gonorrhea, (3) the absence of an opportunity, and (4) the consequence of bad luck—pregnancy. Of course, the risk of syphilis and gonorrhea was always present, but this was the first time in my life that the opportunity presented itself. I could feel a stirring in my loins. I hoped it was not visible.

Odysseus recognized that pleasures could be deadly. When I read the Odyssey, I was intrigued that Odysseus figured out a way to experience the song of the Sirens and live to enjoy that memory. I didn't have a plan to avoid reasons 1 and 2 above, so I moved on.

I resisted these NYC opportunities throughout my senior year in high school, though I went back to the Metropole Cafe a few times to test my resolve. There was no sex in my high school years. I don't count autologous sex, though autologous sex safely addressed reasons 1, 2, and 4.

It may sound strange to some, but I decided to ask my parents at what age it was appropriate to have sex. The first answer I got was "When you are old enough for marriage." I replied that Dad had a friend who married in his forties. Mom released me of all guilt about having sex before marriage when she said, "Something is wrong if you wait until you are forty." I interpreted that answer to mean that when I was ready, I would know it. I was ready, but I still needed to deal with the absence of an opportunity. Then I went to college.

Freshman college guys did not meet my expectation of college life. This was a time when we were supposed to discover our passion and build a successful foundation for a career—by studying. It was time to apply ourselves, but those guys in my dorm at Union College in Schenectady, New York, spoke about sex more often than I thought about it. I remember one guy saying if you hadn't screwed a woman by the end of your freshman year, it probably meant you were homosexual. This was 1965, so the word gay had a very different meaning.

If that guy's theory was right, despite all those daydreams of sex with half the girls in my high school English class, it may be that I was homosexual. I had to do something about this in the next few months. I decided I was going back to the Metropole Cafe.

Paul was a close friend in my freshman year in college. I shared with him my plan for the Christmas break. Being very self-centered, I never wondered about Paul's attitude toward sex. I just sought encouragement to go through with my Metropole plan. Paul caught me by surprise when he told me he could make it easy for me. "Here is an address and a phone number," he said. "Her name is Rosie, and she would be happy to see you." I was shocked to learn that a second student in my freshman class also knew Rosie. Paul said to bring ten dollars.

I did it. E train under the East River and then straight to Rosie's apartment. She gestured for me to lie on the bed. I was obedient. She undressed. The next thing I remember was the E train ride home. I was seventeen years and nine months old and unequivocally heterosexual. With that problem solved, it was time to study for finals.

The Top of the Sixes

In 1964 in New York City, there was a restaurant called the Top of the Sixes. It was on the forty-first floor of the Tishman Building at 666 Fifth Avenue. David Hodes, my only high school friend (who I still see to this day), joined me there when we were seniors in high school.

When the restaurant closed in September 1996, the *New York Times* published an article that attempted to explain why many people felt sad about its death.[*] The author, David Stout, offered this to explain the nostalgia: "Was it unabashed longing for their own lost youth and a time when the ideal car had tail fins that made it look like a fire truck on muscle pills?" He mentioned the view, which was spectacular at a time when restaurants on top of skyscrapers were a novelty. He quoted David Grant, a spokesman for Sumitomo of Tokyo, the building's owners: "Nobody ever went there for the food," but "people proposed to their wives there." Grant recalled that the definition of going to "the city" for many people meant journeying from Queens to Manhattan. That is just what David Hodes and I did.

---

[*] See "No More Tables for Two at the Top of the Sixes," *New York Times*, September 18, 1996.

People went to Top of the Sixes in large numbers. It was the romance and the view. During the week they served their ten millionth meal, a restaurant reviewer described the beef stroganoff as reminiscent of airline food. The *New York Times* subsequently published an article in which a reviewer stated Top of the Sixes was "the sort of place you visit in order to say you've been there, once." David and I went for the cherries jubilee dessert.

At the age of seventeen, I was a bit uncomfortable walking into the restaurant with no intention of having dinner. I asked the maître d' if he would permit the two of us to have dessert. We couldn't afford a full dinner. He said our timing was good, and we got a table by a window. I didn't think dining could get much better than this.

Cherries jubilee contains a liqueur, and yes, I was underage. In New York City in 1964, you had to be eighteen to drink. You could drive at seventeen if you took driver's education and passed the written and practical examinations. Cherries jubilee is flambéed, so when the alcohol is burned, the ethanol reacts with oxygen, forming heat, carbon dioxide, and water. Not all the alcohol is converted to CO_2 and water, though. We broke the law and loved it.

Please permit me to veer off the road of my cherries jubilee story and into the New York state law about driving at the age of seventeen. Many states permitted driving at sixteen, but not New York—unless you had a special dispensation granted to those who passed the driver's education course. David and I both took the course and had no trouble with the written part. But during the practical, David hit a car. When he told me about it, I felt terrible. First of all, hitting a car sounded really scary. Hitting a car during your driver's test was unimaginable.

Before the test, David's biggest concern was how much trouble he'd had during practice sessions with parallel parking. To receive a passing grade, parallel parking was a required maneuver. David told me his parallel parking was perfect during the driver's test. He had backed into that spot without even needing to move forward to straighten out the car. He asked later if I thought his parking performance could overcome the demerit of getting into an accident. I was honest and told him I suspected that getting into an accident during your driver's test automatically disqualified you. It did. He failed on his second try too, but without an accident. Then he passed the test and spent the summer after high school as a taxi driver. As a cabbie, he got into one other accident. Eventually, he became a pulmonologist—one of the most challenging of medical specialties.

Back to cherries jubilee. The flambé sauce is poured over vanilla ice cream. You enjoy the heat from the sauce, the cold of the vanilla bean ice cream, and the sweetness of the cherries. I asked David if he thought we would bring our brides to Top of the Sixes for cherries jubilee. I wondered what my bride would look like. I even asked him if he thought our prom dates would be our brides. The answer to the prom date question was no. But I still wondered who would be the one to "smite" me, as in make me smitten by her beauty inside and out.

I was hit by what I call the delayed thunderbolt, a variant of the thunderbolt that Mario Puzo describes in his novel *The Godfather*. "You can't hide the thunderbolt," he wrote. "When it hits you, everybody can see it. Christ, man, don't be ashamed of it, some men pray for the thunderbolt. You're a very lucky fellow." It took a long time, but I eventually became a very lucky fellow.

David Hodes with me at the Ritz-Carlton in New York, January 2016.

Not My Finest Moment

Until I reached fifth grade, I thought education was an option one chose from a short list of choices: Option 1 was play. Option 2 was education. So when I got home from school around 3:00 p.m., I chose option 1. Homework was placed under the category of education, and that was not the option I chose.

After a while, I noticed the other kids knew a lot more than I did. They could spell words and read. When my parents recognized what was happening to me in school, things changed around the house. There was a lot less playing. I remember once asking my dad if I was smart enough to go to college. He said, "If you study, you will go to college." I didn't believe him at first.

Then the teaching began, as I mentioned in "The Sobbing Sofa" essay. Dad was in charge of science and math. Mom oversaw my education in poetry. She reviewed with me the poets Richard Lovelace, Sir John Suckling, and Robert Herrick ("Gather ye rosebuds while ye may . . ."). Let me embarrass myself with an illustration of the kind of poem that required Mom's tutoring. Here is "Encouragements to a Lover" by Sir John Suckling:

> Why so pale and wan, fond lover?
> Prythee, why so pale?
> Will, when looking well can't move her,
> Looking ill prevail?
> Prythee, why so pale?
> Why so dull and mute, young sinner?
> Prythee, why so mute?
> Will, when speaking well can't win her,
> Saying nothing do't?
> Prythee, why so mute?
> Quit, quit, for shame! This will not move,
> This cannot take her;
> If of herself she will not love,
> Nothing can make her:
> The devil take her!

Mom was most patient with me. Eventually, I learned to love poetry. Today I would summarize "Encouragements to a Lover" with a question: Why are you having so much trouble understanding she is just not into you? Of course, I am a hopeless romantic and would not give up just because she didn't understand we belonged together.

One day in eleventh grade, the junior year in high school, my English teacher had the entire class write an original poem. One of the students asked if there could be an alternate assignment for those who couldn't write poetry. This was a great question. The teacher reminded us that this class was Honors English, and each of us must write a poem. I couldn't do it.

Then I did something I am ashamed of to this day. Mom told me her brother, Julie, wrote her a poem for her sweet sixteenth birthday. I took the original poem, rewrote it in my handwriting, and submitted it for the assignment. I hadn't taken a course in ethics yet.

When the teacher distributed the papers back to the students, she said one submitted poem was copied from another poet's work. She said she had read this poem before, and she knew it was not the student's work. I raised my hand and asked if she was talking about the poem I handed in. In front of the entire class, she said yes.

I decided not to confess.

"You never read this before," I said instead. "This is the first time you've ever read that poem. If you can find the poem anywhere, I will accept an F for the class. But if you cannot locate this in your archives or library [there was no internet in 1963], I will accept an A, and no apology is needed."

I was sixteen. Even now, I wonder about my behavior that day. I was probably angry with myself for cheating on the assignment. I got an A in the class.

Julie gift
for my sweet
Sixteen!

A beggar stood before the gates.
One moment to decide —
And ere the sleepy sentry woke
The beggar was inside

In to the princess' glorious room
He walked, all stealth aside.
His head was high, his mien was proud
His gait his clothes belied

"What meaneth this," the
princess cried.

I bear a
Which have
The beggar
Full twenty
With other gifts than this
prince gone
Yet she remembers
best of all
The Prince who stole a

My uncle Julie's original handwritten poem to my mother for her sixteenth birthday.

FOUR

College

Physical Education: A College Requirement

There is a scene in the first few minutes of the movie *Jumanji: Welcome to the Jungle* in which a studious high school female complains about gym class. She questions the gym teacher about the purpose of the class and says, "Gym is not going to get me into Princeton." The only thing worse than the requirement to take gym in high school is the requirement to take gym in college!

My freshman year in college was spent in Schenectady, New York, at Union College. In 1964, Union College was for men only. I figured that would be the most appropriate environment for a premed student. I was wrong about that. But that's another story. The issue I faced during orientation week was the gym requirement. It was possible to "place out" of gym, but several upperclassmen said they had never met anyone who had.

To place out in a subject I believed would not help me get into medical school, I had to choose two sports and show proficiency in both. That sounded simple, and I planned to place out of swimming and handball. Though I could not "letter" in handball during my Jamaica High School years, I reasoned that showing proficiency should be less difficult than getting a major J (that's *J* for Jamaica).

Gym proficiency testing had a purpose. We were to show that we had the ability to stay physically active our entire lives. Somehow, this could be proved with swimming and handball. Placing out of swimming meant the student had to meet the qualifying time for the swim team in a fifty-yard race. I could not do this, but to my delight, there was one exception to the rule. You automatically showed proficiency in swimming if you had proof of an active Red Cross lifeguard certification. I had spent the summer as a lifeguard at Wel-Met Camps and earned this certification before college orientation. I was proud of that achievement and carried the certificate with me all the time. It was the size of a driver's license.

To demonstrate proficiency in handball, the student had to beat a gym teacher in a match. The first player to score 21 points was the winner. However, the winner had to score at least 2 points more than an opponent. In case of a tie at 20–20, 21 points would not be enough to win. You needed one more.

That game was exciting for me. And it was close. I am sure my passion for the game was evident. I tied the match at 20–20. We exchanged a few serves, but finally, the gym teacher led by a point and was serving. I remember making a difficult shot in the back of the court that just reached the wall. But then the teacher just lightly tapped the ball, and I had no chance of running the full length of the court for a return shot. I lost.

I was gracious about the loss. I may have even looked proud of my accomplishment, though it fell short of the goal. My sweat showed, and I had given it my all. It just wasn't enough. I shook his hand and said thank you. We left the court.

I don't know how to explain the ecstasy of receiving my schedule for the first semester. Swimming was listed under physical education. Next to swimming was a red stamp: "Proficient." And next to handball was another red stamp: "Proficient." I did it. He passed me even though I had lost.

I will always believe it was my passion that got me the passing grade. And because I placed out of gym, I had extra time to study. Maybe that's how I got into medical school.

That College Dream

We all dream, and many of us may have the same dream with a slight variation. Mine is about an economics final exam in college.

I graduated from the University of Michigan in 1968, but I still have that economics dream. I really did take economics in my senior year. I found it captivating. Decades after graduation, I still read articles and books that teach the importance of economics in our historical approach to risk. My favorite is *Against the Gods: The Remarkable Story of Risk* by Peter L. Bernstein. Yet I chose the best career for me—medicine. Economics would have been much tougher.

Perhaps that is one reason the dream keeps recurring. I did OK in the class. But in the recesses of my hippocampus, I must have really been worried about it.

Leaving for Union College in Schenectady,
New York, in September 1964.

Every year or so from the 1960s into the 1970s, I would dream that the economics final was the next day, and I was not prepared. In the dream, I never attended a single class but was informed the day before the exam that I was enrolled and could not drop the course.

I sometimes pulled all-nighters before a final exam. I would do it even in the dream, figuring I could get through Samuelson's classic textbook *Economics* in one night.

As the dream continues, the clock is moving faster than I am turning the textbook pages. I soon realize I cannot finish it before the exam begins. I awake a bit sweaty with my heart racing. Then I realize I already graduated! There is no examination for me to take. And that feels so good. The feeling of relief lasts several hours.

I had gone over a decade without the dream, but just when I thought my hippocampus had matured and resolved all conflicts, a variation of the dream occurred. On the night of December 2, 2019, while at a meeting in DC, I dreamed of a final exam in European history. The dream was frustrating because I was distinctly aware that I got an A in both European history courses in my freshman year. But in the dream, I was a senior, and that freshman course didn't count.

This time, I was able to get through the entire textbook. Somehow, I memorized it all and was ready. I got to the exam room in plenty of time. Then the professor said there would be a change in the examination format. It was to have been an all-essay test, which would have been great because I could regurgitate anything from the textbook word for word. But now the test was one hundred multiple-choice questions, and the topics were not covered in the book.

One of the students asked if the questions were meant for a different class. The instructor replied that the test would be easy for anyone who attended the class this semester. That student didn't attend a single class, and neither did I.

Once again, I got sweaty and tachycardic but then woke up to relief. I was seventy-two at the time and had never had a history final dream before. Yet I bet this will not be the last time I confront the history nightmare.

FIVE

Medical School

How to Choose a Medical Career

When I entered medical school in September 1968, my plan was to make a significant contribution to mankind. The earth would be a safer place with my service. Of course, I had no idea what this contribution would be. That didn't bother me. How was I supposed to know before I had my education, training, and experience?

I remember thinking in my freshman year that medicine was too complicated for anyone to know it all. I had a discussion with one of my classmates expressing my concern that one cannot achieve competency in medicine now or in the future. The scope of medicine was too broad, and the magnitude of information was expanding at an exponential pace.

"Haven't you figured this out yet?" my classmate said to me. "No one can be competent in any one field. There is no such thing as a competent internist or surgeon. What you need to do is pick one disease, and that's it!"

Pick one disease! That seemed really boring in 1968. He then went on to tell me he had already picked his disease, sarcoidosis. I commented that no one knew the cause of sarcoidosis and no one knew how to treat it. He said that made it a perfect choice. I guess he figured he would know more about sarcoidosis than anyone in the world. At the time, I was sure choosing one disease for a career was a pathetic way to approach medical training.

But I needed to choose a specialty. Early on, I chose surgery. Surgery has a special appeal because it offers immediate rewards—especially trauma surgery. Imagine a patient in relatively good health. One drunken driver, and an entire future becomes precarious. The trauma surgeon (with a team of specially trained nurses, technologists, and ancillary support) gives this victim a second chance. Second chances are beautiful things.

Surgery can often reverse an unhealthy medical condition completely. If you have appendicitis, an appendectomy puts you back to square one—where you want to be. If you have Crohn's disease, it's a lifetime of medical care. The internist takes on Crohn's disease. The surgeon takes on appendicitis. Surgery seemed perfect—until my trauma rotation.

Dr. Alexander Walt was chairman of the Department of Surgery at Wayne State University in Detroit for twenty-two years. He served as an honorary, endowed, or distinguished lecturer at universities and medical centers throughout the world. He was president of the American Board of Medical Specialties and the American College of Surgeons, the highest honor accorded to a surgeon.

Perhaps it is no surprise that such a respected surgeon worked in Detroit, which was one of the cities where a new specialty, trauma medicine, first emerged. On January 2, 1972, the *Detroit Free Press* reported 690 killings in the city in 1971. That number was up from the 550 homicides in 1970.

When I walked into the OR in 1971 as part of my trauma rotation, I saw that Dr. Walt had already opened a trauma victim's abdomen and was suturing perforations in the small bowel caused by a bullet wound. He recognized me as a fourth-year medical student at Wayne State and made room for me at the table. When he was finished in the abdomen, he said to me, "Close the case; I will watch you." This was my chance to impress the chairman.

Interns, residents, and medical students often used Ethicon silk suture to practice the art of tying a surgical knot. In our breakroom, I often saw a braid of knots hanging from the arm of a chair—the visual evidence of the need to practice the art. I didn't practice. Now it was time to close the patient.

I mentally graded myself after I finished my work in the OR and awaited the assessment of Dr. Walt. I was pleased with my performance. Then, politely and sincerely, Dr. Walt said, "I would like you to choose another specialty." When I asked why, he said I had the knowledge and the commitment, but I was too slow to be a surgeon. That was enough for me to abandon the dream of surgery as a career. I was impressed with my speed and pleased with the closure. But if the chair says choose another specialty, the only thing I can be sure about is that I won't be a surgeon.

The pathology rotation that followed was interesting. I didn't feel the passion at first. But I was a good airplane spotter—good at pattern recognition. The turning point came when a resident asked me to review a lymph node biopsy with him. The slide was just stained and cover-slipped. He dropped the slide under my microscope and asked me what it was. In about five seconds, I said it was lymphocyte-depleted Hodgkin's disease. He looked at me in awe and said, "Wait

The author with two of the medical world's luminaries, Charles Horace Mayo and William James Mayo. The statues of the brothers are outside the famed clinic in Rochester, Minnesota, that bears their name.

a minute. This diagnosis has huge implications for this patient. Take your time and look again." I looked again. Then I turned back to him and asked if he had just told me to take my time. He had. I found my specialty.

Since that day, I have learned that my classmate was right about choosing one disease. In 2006, I was diagnosed with chronic lymphocytic leukemia (CLL) that was behaving like a diffuse small-cell lymphocytic lymphoma. Thomas Kipps, a University of California, San Diego (UCSD) oncologist, had chosen CLL/lymphoma as his disease. That turned out to be a great decision for me. I've been in remission since 2007.

At my self-made dissecting table in 1961.

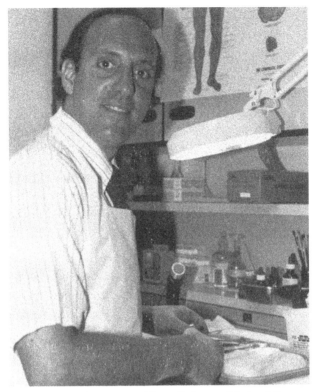

At the surgical cutting table at Palomar Medical Center in the late 1970s.

Sistine Chapel

My obstetrics and gynecology (ob-gyn) rotation in 1971 turned out to be a test of stamina. I wasn't used to working twenty-four hours straight several times a month. This was supposed to prepare me for internship, when we all worked twenty-four hours straight every third night. I was starting to wonder if I belonged with these guys. Richard Geller, whom I met during my internship year, told me he had a problem with working twenty-four hours every third night. He said that meant we miss two-thirds of the good stuff. I just didn't fit this mold.

I hadn't rotated through pathology yet, so my destiny was still obscure. Ob-gyn had the advantage of usually experiencing a happy ending. After my medicine rotation, this thought had a certain appeal. Medical students are obsessed with achieving an acceptable level of competency as defined by the faculty. For many of us, this meant a complete focus on outcome. While outcome is important, safety demands a certain pace to keep risk to a minimum. For example, when performing fluoroscopic procedures, outcome must be balanced against the length of time a patient is exposed to radiation.

Fluoroscopy provides a continuous X-ray image on a monitor. It also provides the patient with a continuous exposure to X-rays. Even those health care providers assisting with the procedure need to be protected, and the chance of adverse events increases with increasing exposure time. Speed is important. And the physicians who perform procedures best are usually fast.

Unfortunately, speed is one of my limitations.

Speed is relevant in ob-gyn too. Emergency cesarean section requires the doctor to remove the newborn from the uterus in about fifteen to twenty minutes. I wondered if practice and commitment would result in great outcomes and acceptable speed. First, I thought I needed a good mentor. Then I realized I needed a different specialty.

My career-changing event occurred in an ob-gyn clinic. My patient was returning because she had a previously abnormal Pap smear. This means dysplasia (a precancerous condition) or squamous cell cancer. If dysplasia is left unattended, it will progress to squamous cell cancer of the cervix.

At the time I was caring for this patient, scientists didn't know that dysplasia and squamous cell cancer were caused by human papillomavirus (HPV). You get the virus through vaginal intercourse, though transmission is also effective via anal and oral sex. Today, a vaccine can prevent HPV, but my patient was born before it was available, and the vaccine is worthless once you have dysplasia. I had to biopsy the suspicious area on her cervix so the pathologist could tell me the diagnosis.

Today, an abnormal Pap smear with dysplasia is followed by colposcopy, a procedure that closely examines the cervix for disease. In the 1970s, we painted the cervix with an iodine solution (Lugol's iodine). A normal cervix absorbed the iodine and looked brownish.

But any white or pale areas could be premalignancy or outright cancer. These are the areas to biopsy.

My patient was prepared for the Lugol's solution. After a careful visual examination, I gently applied it, being careful not to stain the patient's clothes (or my own). Suddenly, my meticulous work was interrupted by Dr. Tommy Evans, who I believe was the chair of the department. He hovered over my shoulder and watched my performance until he yelled in a voice that was heard throughout the clinic, "Kolins, this ain't the Sistine Chapel. Get moving!" I was lucky I discovered pathology.

Wash Your Hands

The importance of handwashing has been known since the days of Dr. Ignaz Semmelweis, a Hungarian physician who promoted the antiseptic technique. He has been described as the "savior of mothers," since he showed how handwashing decreased maternal death from childbirth to less than 1 percent. However, Dr. Semmelweis's colleagues thought him "more than two standard deviations out" when he recommended that obstetricians wash their hands with an antiseptic solution (chlorinated lime solution) prior to delivery.

Semmelweis also showed that maternal mortality rates were three times higher for his obstetrical (OB) colleagues than for midwives. Nonetheless, the medical establishment rejected his ideas. It should be stated that at the time of Semmelweis's recommendation, Louis Pasteur and Joseph Lister had not yet proposed the germ theory of infection. Think about practicing medicine in the early nineteenth century without germ theory. Then imagine someone explaining that there are little things we cannot see or feel (bacteria) that are always found on our hands. These little things can kill a patient. That may indeed have sounded a few standard deviations out.

We all agree today that the surgical scrub is a required infection-prevention practice. In 1971, my OB rotation required just one method for handwashing, the five-minute timed scrub, and I was meticulous about it.

It was fear that accounted for my obsessive-compulsive attitude. On my earlier surgery rotation, I had witnessed a living nightmare. A student left the scrub station about thirty seconds early. The attending surgeon witnessed this deviation from practice and immediately removed him from the rotation. I am not sure where this guy was sent, but surely this was the equivalent of being sent to the principal's office in high school. There were rumors he would not be permitted to finish his training. I imagined four years of college and four years of medical school and a medical career ending with a four-and-a-half-minute scrub.

So when an OB nurse yelled to me one day, "Get into this room! Your patient is about to deliver!" I just couldn't leave the scrub station. I explained that I had two full minutes remaining in my five-minute scrub. The nurse pleaded again and insisted that the baby's head was visible, and I was expected to be in the room for the delivery. I reasoned that I was also expected to complete a five-minute scrub. I wasn't going to be sent to the principal's office.

Two minutes later, I darted into the delivery room and found my patient in the stirrups, lifting up her newborn and handing her to me. I took the newborn, passed her to the nurse, cut the umbilical cord, and successfully delivered the placenta. I remember thanking this multiparous woman for her assistance. I suggested she join me on my rotation. This pleased the OB nurse whose body language now suggested forgiveness. The patient seemed so happy about her new addition to the family that I was surely not going to be reported to the authorities. And I was still in medical school. This was a good day.

Dr. Paul Sweda

A curriculum transformation swept through medical education in the 1960s, but at the Wayne State University School of Medicine, which I entered in 1968, the focus was traditional. The rite of passage required about seven hundred hours of gross anatomy. We were introduced to the subject in a lecture hall by Dr. Nicholas Mizeres, professor of anatomy, who simply announced, "Class, this is gross anatomy." His tone distinctly carried the message: "No one proceeds to the clinical years without passing my class."

Hundreds of hours were spent on dissection. There were four students to a cadaver. Paul Sweda and I worked together some of the time. The requirement for freshman medical students today is fifty-six regular lecture hours and ninety-six laboratory hours. I am not sure what the students do with the five hundred extra hours of education time, but in 1968, the hours and work we put in showed on the first part of the National Board of Medical Examiners test, given after the second year of medical school; the second part came after the fourth year; and the final part came after the internship year.

I don't remember much from those seven hundred hours now that fifty-one years have passed. But I don't remember much of my calculus either, and I got an A in that class. I like to believe I would learn it again faster than I did the first time, but I have no interest in determining if that assumption is correct.

What I remember today is my obsession with viewing all required anatomic structures that the syllabus demanded. When we got to the leg, I couldn't locate the sural nerve. My obsessive-compulsive behavior prevented me from leaving the dissecting table until I had made this identification.

The sural nerve is a sensory nerve in the calf region of the leg. It is made up of branches of the tibial nerve and the common fibular nerve; it courses from the midcalf down to the ankle. An identification at any point along the path would permit me to leave the lab for dinner.

I didn't starve. Paul was in the lab. Paul has spoken many memorable lines to me, and one of my favorites is when he explained his approach to college. He told me he wanted to graduate with the lowest A grade possible. He didn't quite accomplish that because he graduated from Michigan State University with the highest B grade possible. Yet I bet his college experience was more fulfilling than mine. He probably could have been Phi Beta Kappa, but Paul would have considered that time poorly spent.

On another occasion, Paul told me he knew how to solve the world's problems. I couldn't resist asking him to explain.

PAUL: Just repeal Gregor Mendel's laws of inheritance.
JERRY: What! Never mind that you cannot do that. Even if you could, how would that help matters?
PAUL: We need the color of human offspring to be a random event. We need racial features to be random instead of inherited. This way, two Black people could give birth to a white person. Two Asians could give birth to a Black person. It's hard to hate your own.

I have never forgotten that solution because if he could pull it off, I think it would work!

Paul did pull off the sural nerve magic that day in the lab. I didn't think he could find that nerve, but I was hungry for dinner. I asked Paul to break away from his conversation with an assistant, Art Jackson, with whom he often spent considerable time, and help me.

My lack of confidence in Paul probably came from his outwardly casual approach to gross anatomy. He was just so cool and calm. But he came over, I briefed him on my dissection, he looked at the textbook, and in about sixty seconds, he identified the nerve. The professor confirmed the identification, and dinner was immediately scheduled.

Another Paul Sweda event is my absolute favorite, and I'm pissed off that Paul has no recollection of it. The encounter is so vivid in my mind that it is difficult for me to believe he has forgotten it. My son offered an explanation: perhaps the event was nothing special to Paul. Here is what happened:

It was the late 1960s. Civil rights protest marches were common. Big changes were happening in the United States. Wayne State University students joined a protest march that, as I recall, was more of an awareness march on the responsibility of hospitals to care for the indigent population in the community. I am pretty sure this was a slur toward the Henry Ford Hospital because recent news hadn't painted that organization's commitment to the community in a favorable light.

My presence infuriated someone from Henry Ford. I cannot recall any instigation on my part other than being there. He came at me and grabbed the collar of my shirt. I looked up. He was big, mean, and angry.

Did you ever see the movie *Cat Ballou?* In one scene, the Lee Marvin character is upset with a fellow thief. He grabs him by the shirt and says something like "I am going to give you a great gift. I'm going to give you the gift of pain." I was sure I was about to receive this great gift when, out of nowhere, Paul appeared. Paul is about six foot four. I am five foot seven on my best day. Paul and the Henry Ford guy were eye to eye. "You want action? I'm your man!" Paul yelled.

I am not skilled enough to explain the look on Paul's face as he stared into the eyes of the aggressor, but I am familiar with the phrase "If looks could kill." Well, that was the look! The outcome was peaceful. The Henry Ford guy backed away, offering an apologetic gesture. I even remember this guy giving Paul a look that was interpreted by me as "Let's not get too excited over this; I am leaving now."

And I felt wonder—not pain. It was wonder-full.

Detroit: No Place for Wimps

Sometime in the 1990s, my brother, Mark, gave my son, Jeremy, a T-shirt with bold red letters stating "Detroit—No Place for Wimps." This exclamation rings true for me to this day. *Merriam-Webster* defines *wimp* as "a weak, cowardly, or ineffectual person." Does it take courage to live and work in Detroit? I would say it takes resolve.

I lived and worked in Detroit for four years. I attended medical school at Wayne State University and lived within walking distance of the Basic Sciences Building. I didn't need to drive much until the clinical rotations in the third and fourth year. That brings me to one of my favorite "No Place for Wimps" story.

Doug Jackson, a now retired orthopedic surgeon, did his clinical rotation in 1971 at a hospital near I-94, where he once got a flat tire. I would have sought roadside assistance, but that would have been unheard of for an orthopedic surgeon in the making.

Doug removed the jack from the trunk of his car and began the task of changing the tire. In the midst of this undertaking, a car pulled off the interstate and abruptly stopped on the shoulder near Doug's car. The driver leaped out, got into Doug's car, and started ripping

Dr. Paul Sweda.

out the radio. "What are you doing?" Doug said as he confronted the man. Our intruder remarked, "You can have the tires; I just want the radio!" No place for wimps.

When I was in the Public Health Service at the National Institutes of Health (1974–77), the federal government and state of Michigan permitted individuals to maintain residency in the state in which they enlisted. I was still a Michigan resident, so when my driver's license approached its expiration date, I went back to the Department of Motor Vehicles in Detroit. I chose an extended weekend so I could take in a University of Michigan football game. Friday was set aside for the DMV. The line was long, and I was impatient, but I still had a sense of humor. The police suddenly entered the DMV and pushed me aside, and with one quick flick of the wrist, the guy in front of me was handcuffed, pulled out of the line, and hauled off. My lucky day; the wait time had just become shorter.

I had earlier lessons regarding the resilience you need to live in Detroit. In the fall of 1968, my first year of medical school, students were required to buy their own microscopes. I had a Zeiss because I believed it was the best. There would be no scrimping on the tools needed for an education. I eventually took that microscope to San Diego, where I passed the board examination in anatomic pathology given by the American Board of Pathology in 1975.

Monte, who was in my freshman class, didn't get to keep his microscope for long. In the first semester, someone broke into Monte's Detroit apartment. It may have been more than one person. Monte was there with his microscope. They tied Monte up, pushed him under the bed, and stole his microscope. No place for wimps.

That story is hard to forget because the next day at the Basic Sciences Building, Monte saw one of the guys who had tied him up trying to sell his microscope to another medical student! I was told that the police arrested the thief. I like to believe Monte got his microscope back.

Back in those days, I owned a Plymouth Valiant. Not surprisingly, the Valiant was a dark Michigan blue. This used car cost me $600, and it was retrofitted with a four-speed manual Hurst transmission. It almost got me through the four years of medical school until I replaced it with a new pea-green Chevy Nova that cost $2,000.

During one of my clinical rotations, the battery in the Valiant was stolen in a parking structure adjacent to the hospital. In those days, the latch that opened the hood of the car was under the hood itself and not connected to any lock release near the dashboard. That permitted easy access to the engine and car battery for both owner and burglar. I got a new battery and a lesson from a native Detroiter.

The person who had stolen the battery was one of the few people in the world who knew that the blue Valiant would have a brand-new battery the next day. A classmate asked me about my plan to prevent the new battery from being stolen. While I couldn't lock the hood from inside, he explained that I could coat my new battery in Vaseline. My classmate described the dilemma facing the thief who opened the hood of a car and found the battery covered in two inches of grease. Would he steal it, or would he take the battery in some other car? I bought several jars of Vaseline, and the battery stayed with me until the Nova arrived.

In *Tombstone*, a 1993 western, Wyatt Earp (Kurt Russell) and Doc Holliday (Val Kilmer) are depicted taking on the bad guys at the O.K. Corral and elsewhere. My brother and his wife, Maria, got a taste of that feeling while they lived in Detroit. Coming out of a grocery store on East Jefferson Avenue, they walked into a cross fire just like Wyatt Earp did by the riverside forest. And like Wyatt, Mark and Maria lived to tell about it.

Scary. No place for wimps.

Jeremy after high school football practice wearing his "Detroit—No Place for Wimps" T-shirt.

SIX

Internship and Residency

The Spleen

graduated from medical school in May 1972. On July 1 of that year, I started my internship at Massachusetts General Hospital (MGH), where the internship-matching program had sent me. In some ways, it was a match made in hell. I really didn't belong. Some people just love Boston; I loved leaving it on July 1, 1974. But in 1972, I needed to adjust to a new style.

The residents and faculty were talented. Some were even civil. Many thrived on the Socratic method of education (with a Boston variation that caught me by surprise). Basically, the Socratic method has been described as a cooperative argumentative discussion between individuals seeking to learn the truth. But if you found yourself on the wrong side of the argument, enlightenment was not your reward. Instead, one experienced a form of humiliation that translated to "unworthy as a physician."

I remember being in a small group of interns when our Austrian professor asked us to describe our approach to working up a patient with suspected thyroid disease. One of the interns (also called first-year residents) immediately started to share his knowledge. I will readily admit I did not have at my fingertips the breadth of information, both clinical and historical, that my colleague displayed. I remember thinking that if this kind of knowledge was expected, I wouldn't make it through the first month. After the intern completed his discourse, the professor moved forward with an attack on this young physician's diagnostic plan. The attack terrified me. You may say I am exaggerating, but that intern left the program within one week. To this day, I think of him as a talent who was too sensitive for Boston. Despite the professor's belligerence, I was determined to get through this.

Every month, the *New England Journal of Medicine* publishes a clinical pathologic conference (CPC) in which a physician is asked to stand in front of faculty and students, decipher a clinical enigma, and then provide a final diagnosis. The CPC concludes when a pathologist steps in and pronounces the truth. I was told when I was doing my residency at MGH that the chairman of the Department of Pathology, Dr. Benjamin Castleman, had selected one of my cases for a CPC.

The case was the tragic death of a woman in her twenties. She died of infectious mononucleosis (IM) that involved the brain. Brain involvement is rare in IM and worthy of a CPC. My job was simple: present the case at a morning event known as an "organ recital" and work with a senior resident to sign out the case. My autopsy showed hepatosplenomegaly. Both the liver and spleen were enlarged, as were the lymph nodes. That was the extent of my contribution. The brain, according to protocol, was taken by the neuropathology department. The brain is placed in formalin almost immediately after removal. Then the neuropathology department reliably reports its findings in one to two months.

The next morning, Dr. Castleman called me to the front of the room. I was expected to give a brief summary of the clinical findings and attempt to show how these findings correlated to the diseased organs. As soon as I finished my summary, Dr. Castleman said, "Let's look at the spleen!" The spleen in mononucleosis is usually enlarged, and this was no exception. However, when I searched the container for it, it was not where I had left it the night before. Dr. Castleman was getting impatient and irritated by what appeared to be a disobedient resident. "Show me the spleen!" he demanded. I pulled the liver from the container and offered it as a substitute. The spleen was not to be found. Castleman pushed himself away from the table and walked out. Imagine that. I was standing in front of all the residents and interns with their associated faculty, and the chair of the department walked out and left me there.

After an uncomfortable silence, the chief resident, Bruce Ragsdale, looked at me and said he had a question. "Did you also apply to the Brigham for training?" he asked in reference to another Boston teaching hospital. I said I only applied to MGH. "That's too bad," the chief resident said. And everyone left.

I didn't leave. I wasn't quitting like the talented intern who knew more about thyroid disease than I did. Yet I was mystified. I swear the spleen had been there the night before. I tried my best not to let the "spleen story" define me, but it followed me for quite a while.

I attended what we called "mixers" in the 1970s. Interns and residents from all over Boston met in a casual atmosphere that was enhanced by wine, beer, and liquor. I had my share. I remember an attractive blonde engaging me in conversation. I thought things were going very well until she asked me what hospital I worked in. Of course, I said, "Mass General." She asked if I had heard about the pathology resident who lost the spleen in a fatal case of mononucleosis. I remember my reply vividly. I looked her right in the eye and said with the sternest voice I could muster, "I didn't lose that spleen. It was there the night before I left the hospital." Those were the last words we spoke. I went back to the Harvard School of Public Health dormitory to sleep it off.

By the time I left Boston, I had recovered much of the ground I lost over the spleen incident. That Austrian professor, Dr. Walter Putschar, complimented me in front of the others at the end of the year when I made an irrelevant diagnosis of an enchondroma in a finger. He professed the importance of thoroughness in medicine and used me as an example of commitment to the cause. Obviously, I never forgot that accolade, even though the diagnosis played no role in the care of the patient.

In the early 1980s, while practicing surgical pathology at Palomar Medical Center (PMC) in Escondido, California, Dr. Fred Hammill, a surgeon, performed a lymph node biopsy on a young male. I remember it well because he told me the biopsy was scheduled for 6:00 a.m., and he wanted me there to immediately examine the lymph node. That was the only time in my career when a biopsy was scheduled before 7:00 a.m., but I was there and made a diagnosis of IM. I was less than honest when I said my diagnosis was based on my examination of the lymph node. The microscopic appearance of a lymph node with mononucleosis is not pathognomonic, which means there is no appearance in the lymph node that is unequivocally diagnostic of mononucleosis. What I actually did was a STAT Monospot test to prove my hypothesis and got it right. This test is positive if the patient has been exposed within the preceding six weeks. The surgeon was surprised by my confidence because he had done a Monospot test a few days earlier, and it was negative. For showmanship purposes, I enjoyed not telling him that I had done the test just a few minutes earlier. Instead, I just said to repeat the test because I was sure my diagnosis was correct.

After the case with Dr. Hammill, I did a review of the literature because I was surprised that the Monospot test he had performed was negative. Unexpectedly, I found an article in the *Journal of Neurology, Neurosurgery, and Psychiatry* published by Dr. Fred Hochberg, who was the chief resident of neuropathology at the time I did an "organ recital" on that case of fatal mononucleosis. The article has a picture of the spleen that had gone missing. Beneath the spleen was a metric ruler to assist the viewer in assessing the size of the spleen. Under the ruler was the MGH case number linked to the autopsy. It was the same case number as the autopsy I had performed in 1972. I still have the carbon copy of that autopsy report. Yes, I said carbon copy.

Boston was a tough place for me. I was most pleased to move to the National Institutes of Health (NIH) on July 1, 1974. At the NIH, there are ladies and gentlemen attending to ladies and gentlemen.

Postscript: There is an old saying that you can get a lot of information out of Boston, but you cannot get any information into Boston. I guess that's the arrogant part of the Socratic method. For those who would like to review the autopsy report, it is logged as MGH case no. 36,442.

My neuropathology residency class of 1973–74. I'm in the back row, second from the left. Dr. Fred Hochberg is in the row below me, second from the left. The internationally renowned neurologist and Director of Neuropathology, Dr. Edward Peirson Richardson, is second from the left in the front row.

Seersucker Pants and Redemption

I did about sixty autopsies in 1972–73 during my first year at MGH. One of those cases was of particular interest to the chairman of the department, Dr. Benjamin Castleman. The case involved a patient who had needed a chest tube placed on the right side to treat a pneumothorax. I felt terrible when I opened the patient's chest. According to the case report, the chest tube had perforated "the posterior basal segment of the right lower lobe of the lung." The patient died from complications of the chest tube insertion. Without the insertion, the patient could not live, but in this case, the placement contributed to the patient's demise.

I didn't look at my autopsy discovery as a learning opportunity, even if it was. I kept thinking about the resident who placed the tube. Someone was going to get punished for this error. I don't know how this case was handled; I just presented the findings at the morning organ recital.

Dr. Castleman was excited about my findings. He was smiling and enthusiastic as he taught the internal medicine residents the lessons to be learned. Castleman felt the autopsy room was the place where the dead taught the living. And the lessons kept on coming. Castleman thought the autopsy procedure was so important that he gave a $1,000 reward to the resident who got the most autopsy permissions each year. In 1972, a resident had an annual salary of $10,000. A $1,000 bonus was a 10 percent increase, and it was a motivator. This resulted in a few of us doing over a hundred autopsies in 1972.

I often wondered if the autopsy examination was as valuable as I was being told. It took me over five hours to perform the procedure. I thought about suggesting that the pathology residents offer $2,000 to the physician who got the fewest number of autopsy permits. I kept that thought to myself, although such a reward was not beyond the scruples of some of my colleagues.

I know this because I did an autopsy on a case in which I found only three of the four parathyroid glands. The chief resident told me I was in trouble because the faculty member who was assigned to my case wouldn't sign off on an autopsy if all four parathyroid glands were not examined. I was distraught.

As a pathology resident, you learn that when you are in big trouble, talk to a diener. A diener assists the pathologist in removing the organs of the deceased, thus permitting a thorough examination. I don't remember the diener's name, but he knew the senior faculty assigned to my case.

"You couldn't find all the parathyroid glands, could you?" he asked me.

I admitted that I couldn't, but he said he could help me. I explained that the body had long been released to a funeral home. He took me to the back room and pointed out a jar filled with parathyroid glands.

"How many do you need?" he asked.

"Just one," I answered.

"Here you go."

And the case was signed out without incident.

In the case of the patient with the chest tube lodged in the right lower lobe of the lung, I kept the tube exactly in place as I found it. I thought this would make a good impression on the chairman. At organ recital, I placed the right lung on the table, carefully orienting it so that the tube was lying flat. To do this, I could not place the lung in its normal anatomic position; I had to rotate it ninety degrees.

Dr. Castleman, being a traditional anatomic pathologist, rotated the lung back ninety degrees. As he taught his audience of interns and residents, I slyly rotated the lung back to the position I had originally placed the organ. I thought I was being helpful, but Dr. Castleman was visibly pissed. I tried to interrupt him to explain my actions. But you just don't interrupt the chairman (who shortly thereafter was appointed interim CEO of MGH).

There was nothing I could do. When he rotated the lung that last time, gravity took over. Blood from the lung drained down the chest tube onto his seersucker pants. He walked out in the middle of his teaching exercise. That was the second time in my career

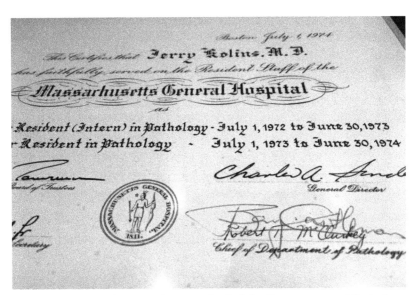

Dr. Benjamin Castleman, who was chief of the Department of Pathology at MGH during my residency there from 1972 to 1974, agreed to cross out the name of his successor and sign his name on my residency certificate.

Dr. Castleman walked out when I was presenting at a morning organ recital. You had to be strong to finish the MGH program.

I left MGH in good standing. In fact, when I moved to San Diego County in 1977, Dr. Castleman left MGH for Stanford. He gave a talk at Stanford, so I flew up to Northern California to hear him. After his talk, I went to him with my residency certificate and showed him that it was signed by his successor—not him. He said this was unacceptable and that I must send it back to MGH to get a fresh certificate that he could sign.

"No, let's not do that," I said. "Why don't you cross out his name and sign your name above your cross-out?"

I have never seen such happiness on this face. I have the signed certificate, complete with the cross-out, framed in my hospital laboratory office.

It proves you can still recover from what seems like an irreversible blunder, like staining the seersucker pants of a leader.

A Portrait of Tolerance

I departed MGH for the NIH on July 1, 1974, the same day the legendary Dr. Benjamin Castleman retired and headed for a position at Stanford. The residents and faculty in his department were given portraits of their chief posed in the world-famous Ether Dome in the Bulfinch Building at MGH. He signed my gift three times, but only one was correct. His first spelling of my last name appeared as *Collins*. I went back to him and carefully explained that about twenty-seven years earlier, I learned my last name was spelled with a *K* and one *l*. He looked a bit perplexed but tossed away the first portrait and signed the second, "To Jerry Kollins with warmest regards." The regards turned from warm to annoyed when I mustered the courage to tell him there is only one *l* in *Kolins*.

I look back at this encounter and recall the "Get Out of Jail Free" card found in the board game *Monopoly*. As a young boy, the concept captured my imagination. Just the thought of being forgiven for some wrong you wish you never committed

An autographed portrait of Dr. Benjamin
Castleman. This is the third one he made for
me because he misspelled my last name on
the first two. But I'm not complaining.

brought on a feeling of peace and comfort. As an adult, I carry around imaginary "Tolerance Cards." I have learned that my aggressiveness and enthusiasm sometimes offend other people. Dr. Castleman appeared somewhat offended. This young resident's persistence bordered on the obnoxious. If I had only one "Tolerance Card" in my quiver, I would have given it to Dr. Castleman on that day.

That's an Abnormal Pancreas

During our senior year in 1972, almost all medical students at Wayne State University in Detroit entered the Internship / Residency Matching Program. A student submitted a list of desired hospitals for internship and resident training. Hospitals prepared a list of their top choices, and a computer made the matches.

I was matched to MGH for residency training in pathology and moved to Boston a few days before July 1, when I was to start. On June 30, I decided that a timed practice run from Harvard student housing to MGH was in order. I certainly didn't want to be late for my first day. I was nervous and wondered if the performance expected of me would match my skill set.

The anatomic pathology training program was intense. I performed my first autopsy on July 8, 1972. It took me six hours to complete the dissection. Ed Beckman, a senior resident, guided me through this first case. He was from New Orleans, had a slight drawl, and came with a style best described as easy and affable. He liked college football.

There was one time I really underestimated Ed. We were at a picnic, and about ten of us decided to play touch football. Ed was quarterback. "Kolins, go long," he said. Usually, that meant "Keep running; you're just a decoy. The play will go elsewhere."

I was not insulted by being assigned the "go long" route; I was happy to be included in the game. Ed dropped back to pass, and I ran. And I ran and ran—like Forrest Gump. When I felt I was out of reach, I assumed the play was over and slowed up. I turned around and saw the ball sail about three feet over my head. If I had kept running, that ball would have hit me on the hands. Ed had advice for me in the autopsy suite, and he had advice for me at the picnic: "You shouldn't have stopped running."

Ed also oversaw the second autopsy I performed, this one on July 12. The case was a four-day-old newborn who had died of diffuse bleeding (disseminated intravascular coagulation) with intracerebral hemorrhage. I brought the hematoxylin- and eosin-stained slides to Ed. When he looked at the pancreas, he asked me for my opinion. I said, "It's a pancreas." Ed told me to look carefully because, he said, "You can see viruses." It was my second week as a pathology resident, and I thought Ed Beckman was giving me a dose of southern humor. "You need an electron microscope to see a virus," I said. Ed took the pointer embedded in the optic field and circled a dense basophilic intranuclear inclusion body. "That's cytomegalovirus [CMV]," he said.

"You can actually see CMV under the light microscope." Once he showed me this, I found those inclusions in the lung, liver, kidney, adrenal glands, and thyroid.

When Ed had thoroughly reviewed the CMV case and my write-up was found to be acceptable, he said Dr. Benjamin Castleman, chair of the Department of Pathology, wanted the case presented as a CPC. All CPC cases are published in the *New England Journal of Medicine*. I thought, *Wow, I'm in my second week, and already we have a publication.*

Yes, I was naïve enough to think that somehow Ed and I would be included in the publication, since I did the autopsy and Ed made the diagnosis. Medicine doesn't work that way. Neither one of us would be mentioned or have a role in the CPC. Instead, a neonatologist was asked to review the record without knowing the autopsy findings and explain his diagnosis to an auditorium filled with physicians. A pathology professor then presented the anatomic findings. You need to be of strong mind and body to be the clinician offering a diagnosis because you are putting yourself in front of the MGH staff, offering your clinical impression, and you could be very wrong. Only the pathologist knows the final diagnosis.

The next time I sat across a microscope from Ed, he told me it was about time that I taught a Harvard medical student. "Put together some slides and teach a freshman something you know," he said. This seemed ridiculous. One month into the program, and I'm teaching Harvard medical students—does this really make sense? Ed just said, "Do it. And do it Bostonian style."

I decided that my first student would be taught from that CMV autopsy case. I showed him a normal pancreas first. Remember when Ed put that slide under the microscope, and all I could see was normal pancreas? My plan was to show the student a normal pancreas and then follow it with the CMV pancreas. I was prepared for the student to make the diagnosis of CMV immediately, then lecture me on the clinical findings in a patient who is infected.

The student looked at the normal pancreas slide and, with an air of confidence, told me that it was from an abnormal kidney. Recalling Ed's directive to handle my first teaching assignment with

"Bostonian style," I said, "Well, as a kidney, it is very abnormal. But as a pancreas, it is just fine."

Teaching students was not so tough after all.

Ed Beckman.

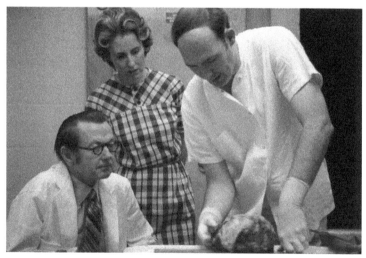

Dr. Ed Beckman at organ recital, presenting to the internationally recognized Dr. Robert Scully with Dr. Vera Hyman observing.

SEVEN

Marriage and Parenting

A First Date Leading to Marriage

Frank Musumici was my dad's partner in business. They formed a financial advisory company that initially focused on commodities and had a seat on the Chicago Board of Trade. The risk associated with this commitment eventually led Frank and my dad to sell the seat and start a more conservative financial business that traded in bonds. I will always remember Frank's advice to me: "You don't have to tell people everything you are thinking; some information can be kept to yourself." Good advice. Sometimes I even followed it.

Dale was a medical technologist at the National Institutes of Health (NIH) Blood Bank and the cutest young thing I ever saw. I once squeezed her thighs under the table while I was giving an anatomy talk during a brain-cutting session. Yes, I brought a brain to the blood bank and had the students gather around. I then cut the brain to demonstrate the anatomy and spoke to the function of various regions within. I often wonder if anyone saw my squeeze under the table. I was captivated.

In 1976, I had an opportunity for a dinner date. I had a place in Bethesda on Pooks Hill Road. Dale came over and made dinner. The menu was designed to win my heart through my stomach. And that strategy worked! I had never tasted freshly baked homemade bread. Just as importantly, I had never tasted a Caesar salad. The bread was magnificent. The Caesar salad was perfection in the kitchen. If you think I am exaggerating, I would add that we've been married for forty-one years, and my excitement over Dale's Caesar salad has only increased over time. Ingredients include raw egg, garlic, olive oil, Grey Poupon mustard, moutarde de Meaux, lemon juice, Parmesan cheese, bacon, and sometimes anchovies. It is easy to list the ingredients, but knowing how much of each is the magic.

The croutons were handmade with garlic and olive oil. The aroma telegraphed the special evening to follow. No matter how the day had gone, the evening would be perfect. Between the bread and the salad, no man could ask for more. It was a Michelin three star.

I was immature and New York arrogant. Everything served had to be perfect. So far, it was. But to Dale, the salad and bread were the introduction. The main event was USDA prime flank steak.

Understand, I am no cook. I know what I like, but being a critic does not seem as impressive as being the creator.

The flank steak was not marinated as it should have been. I didn't know it was not marinated. I just knew this was one very tough steak—not worth the effort to chew it. But no one went hungry. All I needed was the Caesar salad, bread, and wine. That was perfection.

If you are served an entrée and you don't eat it, you have some explaining to do. If you don't like the entrée and appear very happy with the dinner, that can seem weird. It did to Dale. "Don't you like the dinner?" she asked.

This was a crucial question. High emotional intelligence was important here. Unfortunately, I had low emotional intelligence, and I forgot Frank Musumici's advice. I told Dale everything I was thinking.

I could have said it was the best salad I'd ever tasted. I could have added that at more than twenty-five years old, I had never tasted freshly baked homemade bread. That this had been the most amazing dinner ever.

But I didn't say that. Instead, I said, "There is something wrong with the steak."

When I went to work the next Monday at the NIH Blood Bank, Mary Ann Tourault, the blood bank supervisor, asked about the date. I told her everything. She asked me to come into her corner of the lab—her office. Mary Ann pulled a business card from her Rolodex, the clunky-looking wheel of index cards that held the names, addresses, and phone numbers of key people and places. Pre-Apple, pre-Microsoft, preinternet.

Dale Monday Kolins, known for her tolerance and adaptability.

"Here is a number of a florist." She said. "This is your only chance." I didn't realize I was in trouble. I thought it had been a great evening. Mary Ann told me not to be optimistic. Flowers don't always work.

I lucked out. We're planning our forty-second anniversary in Maui. Life is good.

My Kingdom for a Procedure Manual

I am board certified in anatomic pathology, clinical pathology, and blood banking/immunohematology. Our professional lives are guided by procedure manuals. I was chief of staff of Palomar Medical Center (PMC) Escondido. How do you handle a disruptive physician? The secret weapon is the procedure manual. I learned this from Dr. Rick Sheff, who is a consultant to hospital medical staffs that are struggling with physician performance. He told me, "Whenever a problem arises, ask yourself what the procedure manual says."

All too often, my response was "Our procedure manual does not address this point." To that, Rick would say that my assignment was to write the procedure.

That is the catch. Writing a procedure is not easy. Getting support for a procedure is one of life's greatest challenges. And not just for physicians.

I needed a procedure manual for raising my children. I have a not-so-impressive track record. Let's consider the time Dale left me for just three days to fly to Oahu to give a lecture, and my duty was to take care of Jessica, our daughter, who was about three at the time.

"What's the procedure?" I asked. Dale replied that I should wake her up, help her get dressed, and bring her to Gillispie School—that is, preschool. I suggested we keep her in a ponytail for three days and skip the hair-combing step that was part of helping Jessica get dressed. Dale said absolutely not.

I had no procedure manual. I failed these three days. I kept telling myself I have redeeming qualities, but I could not think of any that week.

Once when Dale was pregnant with Jessica, she told me she was exhausted and had to go to sleep. She said that I should put Jeremy, our two-year-old son, to bed at 8:00 p.m. That was the only directive I got. When 8:00 p.m. came around, I told Jeremy it was bedtime and thought he would agree and maybe ask me to read a bedtime story. But he didn't. Instead, he started to reason with me.

"Dad, do you go to sleep when you are not tired?" he asked.

"No, I go to sleep when I am tired."

"Dad, I am not tired. Let's watch TV."

"Okay."

There is never a procedure manual around when you need one. The pathetic part of the story is that I fell asleep watching TV. Jeremy woke up Dale and told her we needed to put Daddy to bed.

One weekend when I was not on call, Jeremy, then three, woke up around the same time I did. He suggested that I make hard-boiled eggs for breakfast. I was excited because I knew how to make hard-boiled eggs. My mom taught me to place the egg in boiling water for twenty minutes, let it cool, and enjoy. I put the pot filled with water on the cooktop.

After about five minutes, Jeremy announced that the eggs were done and we could have breakfast. But I remembered my mom's lesson and insisted the eggs needed fifteen more minutes. "It won't take long," I said. What happened next is legend in our family. Jeremy had a tantrum. He pleaded with me not to ruin breakfast.

After the eggs were in the boiling water for about seven minutes, Jeremy came unglued. "Get the eggs out of that water!" he wailed. I lost my temper and told him I would take the eggs out of the water and serve them if he agreed to eat them no matter what condition they were in. Jeremy said yes. Out came the undercooked eggs.

"Jeremy, do you see what happened here? You should have trusted me," I said.

"Dad, you ruined it," he answered. If I had taken the eggs out at the five-minute mark, Jeremy said, the eggs would have been perfectly hard-boiled. But I had insisted on keeping them in the boiling water for several extra minutes, and during that time, the eggs went from hard-boiled to soft again.

"It's all your fault," my young son told me.

I was speechless. Where is a procedure manual when you need one? Dale told me I could not function in the real world. I agreed.

Hi, Mrs. Kolins

In my early thirties, I read *Is There Life after High School?* by Ralph Keyes. The content of the book is not as important as the question. Sometimes I think the answer accounts for the existence of Facebook. For me, high school was a critical time. It was in high school that I learned my limitations, and that was the best preparation for college. Compared to high school, college was straightforward. So when my son, Jeremy, reached high school, it was a vicarious experience for me.

Jeremy did the things in high school that I couldn't do. He lettered in football. Coming from Jamaica High School in New York City, hearing that someone lettered in football generated a question: How can you letter in high school football? Football was prohibited at Jamaica High School in 1964. I just assumed all good high schools followed Jamaica's example. Turns out, there are many high schools of high caliber with football teams. Amazing!

Jeremy took an acting class with his best friend, Matt Solovay. They performed in *Evita*. I had similar opportunities at Jamaica High School, but fear of failure kept me from acting class. In my defense, I did run for president of the General Organization (that's like high school student president). And I won. That means public speaking was appealing to me, and I enjoyed it—most of the time.

Jeremy achieved a level of performance that was only a dream to me. For example, when he was in the eighth grade, he took the SAT. His score was so high, he was invited to Switzerland in the summer before ninth grade to study mathematics. Wow, I would have loved that.

The only reason I didn't become a mathematician was the limitations imposed by my DNA, although the Kolins family does have a mathematician. My brother Mark's son, Samuel, got a PhD in mathematics from Cornell. When I heard Sam got into Cornell, I told

Mark that Sam must have really aced the Graduate Record Examination (GRE). My brother said I didn't understand. "All the applicants to these schools ace the GRE," he stated. The exceptional students among them were asked to take an even higher-level examination. About this next level exam, my memory is foggy, but as I recall from my brother's description, the test was about three to four hours and had only five to seven questions. I asked Mark how Sam thought he had done.

"Let me put it this way," Mark said. "Three days after the exam was over, Sam came to me and said, 'I just figured out the answer to problem five!'"

Mathematicians have brains that are wired differently than mine. That's why I am a pathologist. I wondered if mathematics was Jeremy's future, but Jeremy heard a different drum. In California, you can drive a car at sixteen. In my opinion, Jeremy enjoyed this freedom at the expense of study. I suspect that even today, Jeremy would say sacrificing study time was not a sacrifice. He was experiencing life, and the experience did not hold him back from a master's degree in accounting and passing the five-part CPA examination on the first try.

During his teenage years, I didn't understand him. He didn't understand me. We both learned the value of tolerance, so some good came of that difficult time.

Jeremy communicated with his friend Matt using some form of email before I had even heard of this technology. In the early email systems, the individuals who wished to communicate with each other needed to be online at the same time. In 1990, Jeremy and Matt were staying in touch via such technology. If the kids weren't on the phone, I assumed they were in their room studying. It never occurred to me that it was possible to chat without a phone.

On one late afternoon, Dale walked into Jeremy's room and saw a communication between Jeremy and Matt. The messages were visible on the computer screen. Dale gently moved Jeremy away from the keyboard and then typed, "Have you finished your homework yet?"

Matt's immediate reply was "Hi, Mrs. Kolins."

They know us better than we know ourselves.

Raising Parents

It is not easy for young kids to take control of their lives. Parents can be domineering and obstinate. Middle school adolescents have minds of their own, as it should be, but they are usually subordinate to the parents. My son knew how to take control. And it took a while before I realized what was happening.

He was around thirteen. I always considered high school the foundation of one's educational experience. Performance in high school influences college admissions committees. There is no substitute for a superb high school education. That was me in 1990. Jeremy was advancing from middle school to high school.

We live in La Jolla, where the Bishop's School is located. It is one of the best. The students who perform well there get into the best colleges and universities in the country. You need to take an entrance examination for admission, and if you get accepted, this is what your parents can look forward to:

Annual tuition for grades six through twelve in 2020–21
   (includes midmorning cereal and hot lunch): $38,310
Estimated books, iPads, and supplies: $600
Estimated uniforms: $350
Incidentals—additional costs related to sports and arts:
   $1,000
Round-trip transportation (optional): $2,725
One-way transportation (optional): $1,750

Wow, is it high school or college?

I was somewhat anxious about Jeremy scoring at a level that would be acceptable to the Bishop's School. My twisted mind thought this was a crucial crossroad in Jeremy's life. I remembered he took the SAT in eighth grade when most kids take it in eleventh or twelfth grade. He scored very well, but the Bishop's School was highly competitive.

Then there was Francis Parker, another very good high school. I had decided Francis Parker was almost as good as Bishop's. My memory on this is somewhat foggy, but I think Dale was familiar with Francis Parker and wanted Jeremy to visit. Certainly no harm in visiting a good "fallback" school.

Each school had applicants take a standardized entrance examination. I was told there was no significant difference between these tests. But one could score at a level that was "passing" for one high school and not for the other.

And that is what happened. Jeremy scored well enough to get admitted to Francis Parker, but he was rejected by Bishop's. I was stunned and disappointed. Jeremy was excited. It appeared that the prospective high school student was ready and willing, and Dad needed psychological support.

After a few days, I still wasn't over it. I called Francis Parker first. Whoever I spoke to mentioned that it was strange for a student to score well enough to be admitted to Francis Parker and not Bishop's. She suggested I check with Bishop's to be sure there was no clerical error. I did. When I spoke with the administrator at Bishop's, my demeanor was quiet and shy. I meekly asked if it would be possible to check if a mistake had been made. To my surprise, the person I spoke with was curious too. She said she would check and call back.

A few days later, I heard from Bishop's. The caller was polite and to the point as she described a strange test result. The test had a hundred questions. The first twelve on Jeremy's were answered and the remaining were blank. The test was timed like the SAT. I said that perhaps Jeremy was too slow in answering the questions to finish. She said that was possible but he'd gotten all twelve correct.

It took another day or two for me to have the courage to ask Jeremy about the Bishop's School entrance examination. It was a calm discussion that went like this:

DAD: Jeremy, was that Bishop's School test tough?
JEREMY: No, not really.
DAD: But they said you only answered twelve questions. I figure it must have been tough if you couldn't finish.
JEREMY: Oh, no. It wasn't tough. I decided not to finish.
DAD: Why not?

JEREMY: I want to go to Francis Parker. If I had finished that test, you would have forced me to go to Bishop's.
DAD (AFTER A SPEECHLESS MOMENT): Oh.

This is what I call raising your parents and taking control. He had me figured out completely. I was going to save his career by forcing him to go to Bishop's. Instead, he saved his own career by not finishing his entrance exam.

Does Dad have any regrets? Only one: I wish Jeremy had handed in his homework more often.

Handing in Your Homework

When I was in third grade, my teacher spoke with my parents during parent/teacher conference week. My parents were told that Jerry did not prepare for class. He did not take homework seriously.

Our class got a spelling test of ten words on Mondays. Anyone who wrote all ten words correctly was exempt from a retest on Friday, when the teacher announced the same words. A passing grade on Friday was 100 percent because the students knew what words would be on the test and should be prepared. My mom and dad were told that Jerry usually got 70 to 80 percent.

Dad came home from the conference and asked me why I didn't tell him about my homework assignments. I said we didn't get homework assignments. I believed that even though these tasks were distinctly assigned to us all. I think my brain separated home from school, and anything that happened at school stayed at school.

Don't make too much fun of me. There is a book titled *The Origin of Consciousness in the Breakdown of the Bicameral Mind* by Julian Jaynes. I am not an expert on Jaynes's thesis, but I think my right brain was directing my left brain. The left side was saying, "We have homework to do. Let's do it." The right side was saying, "Don't listen to that. We work in school, and we play at home." I liked the right brain.

Dad liked the left brain. He started going over my homework with me every night. His goal was to teach me to take it seriously.

Jeremy is still teaching his parents, as this 2017 photo shows.

I protested at first, but it was far less painful to be obedient than to challenge his logic. So I began doing homework. And I started getting 100 percent. That felt good.

I told my dad I liked getting 100 percent. He asked if I would like to do that in all my classes, and I said yes. "Just do as I say," he advised. And I became the "obedient one." And I kept getting 100 percent.

Now comes my son, Jeremy. He didn't hand in his homework, but he actually did it! That killed me. He did the work but did not hand it in for credit. Instead, he got demerits for this behavior.

Can you imagine my frustration? He did the work. When I was his age, I heard my right brain telling me the work was not important. Don't do it. So I didn't do it. Jeremy did it perfectly and then argued that there was no need to hand it in because it was correct; he had learned the material. He reasoned that it was not important that the rest of the world know he had learned the lesson. He knew it, and that was enough.

I was in my forties, and I had a more practical understanding of how grades are given. The teachers had to assume the assignment was beyond Jeremy's capabilities—even though he would be admitted to the University of Michigan and then get a master's degree in accounting from San Diego State University. I didn't understand what was going on in Jeremy's head.

One must have an epiphany to reach serenity, and my ultimate enlightenment arrived when I embraced the fact that I didn't understand the decisions about life that Jeremy has made. I still don't understand them. But I have come to accept the decisions—and that I do not understand them.

Jeremy and I struggled in our relationship, but there was a turning point. After I accepted my lack of understanding, I concluded that my advice to Jeremy about his life should be of interest only when he sought it. I needed to stop trying to have my son live the life I thought I should have lived. He was entitled to his own. As Mercedes said in the movie *The Count of Monte Cristo*, "Edmond, let it go."

And I did. And finally, I am happy and serene in my relationship with my son.

Men Are from Mars, Women Are from Venus

It is remarkable to me that one simple concept—men and women are different—could be turned into a book, but John Gray did it in *Men Are from Mars, Women Are from Venus* in 1992. In the 1980s, many believed there was no significant difference. In fact, if a man tried to explain the difference, he would probably be labeled a chauvinist. That sounded like a dirty word, so I didn't try to explain the difference to anyone—until Gillispie School.

Gillispie is an independent private school in downtown La Jolla. It enrolls students from preschool through sixth grade. It is attractive to parents who want to give their kids a jump-start on life. Gillispie promotes an expertise in education for those age two to twelve.

Parenting has always been mystical to me. Without a procedure manual, my father would have served as a superior substitute—if he didn't live 2,700 miles away in North Miami Beach.

Raising children is a complex problem, as Atul Gawande explains in his book *The Checklist Manifesto*. In summary, he says there are three types of problems: the simple, the complicated, and the complex. A simple problem is one that, once solved, can be easily solved time and time again.

For example, let's say you are searching for the perfect method to make a lemon meringue pie. You try different recipes, and finally, you hit the one approach that is second to none. This problem is solved forever because you can repeat that recipe whenever you want. The complicated problem cannot be solved by one person. Sending a man to the moon and back safely is too complicated for one person to figure out. But with a team of specialists including physicists, engineers, electricians, and construction workers, you can do it. And if you do it once, you can do it again.

The complex problem is infuriating because once it is solved and the process is carefully documented, the solution will never work again. Raising children is a complex problem.

Gillispie was a good decision for our son, Jeremy, and his parents. I was rarely able to leave the hospital in time to pick him up at school. Dale often described me as one who struggles with the real world. I will not challenge that assertion. It made me feel good inside whenever I could pick up Jeremy and drive him home with me. This could only happen before middle school. Things changed fast.

I also remember a few times when I took him to Burger King for breakfast. A nutritionist would be furious because we would indulge in bacon, cheese, and egg croissants of some kind. We were together for a few minutes before surgical pathology overwhelmed me.

On one of those rare afternoons when I left the hospital early, which means before 6:00 p.m., and picked up Jeremy, I was tired, and my guard was down. A mother of a student overheard me telling Jeremy to put down a doll because we had to get going. The mother came over to me with a somewhat condescending air and said there was absolutely nothing wrong with my son playing with dolls.

If I'd had my wits about me, I would have said something like "You are correct; I agree with you." And I did agree with her. But I felt the need to teach her a lesson. I resented the fact that she thought I didn't understand that it was OK for boys and girls to play with dolls. That wasn't a difficult concept. So I told her I didn't mind when my son played with dolls, but I noticed it upset the girls around him because he just wouldn't put them down until he figured out how to remove the head.

To this day, I smile at my approach to this mother because the horror on her face was worth the price of admission to the show. And Jeremy really did play with dolls that way.

Longs Peak in Rocky Mountain National Park

Longs Peak is in the northern Front Range of the Rocky Mountains in Colorado. The mountain was named in honor of the explorer Stephen Harriman Long, and at 14,259 feet, it is one of the four-teeners in Rocky Mountain National Park. According to Wikipedia, the easiest route to the summit is a nontechnical climb during the summer. I chose the Keyhole route during the warmer months. I know my limitations.

I first tried to summit Longs in 1973 and failed. I went too early, the snow was deep, and the ice was treacherous. But in August 1974, all snow and ice were gone. It took me over seventeen hours of hiking, but I made the summit. This was one of the most inspiring physical accomplishments of my life. In 1994, it was time to try it again.

Jeremy was a senior in high school and planned on attending the University of Michigan in August. That summer would be perfect for a father-and-son attempt on the Longs summit. We slept in Estes Park and took a few day hikes before the 2:00 a.m. wake-up on hike day. We were to complete the round trip before sunset, so we had to begin in the dark. We did not prepare as we should have. I showed my age (forty-seven); Jeremy did not have the proper footwear and carried a set of keys on his belt. I remember a hiker asking what he was planning to open when he got to the top.

We ate a high-carbohydrate diet the night before and got to the trail by 3:00 a.m. The hike from the trailhead (at 9,405 feet) to the summit is 8.4 miles with a total elevation gain of 4,875 feet. The tough part of the climb begins at Boulder Field, 6.4 miles in. I videotaped some of the climb. My breathing rate was scary at the summit, though I didn't know this until we returned and I watched the video.

We hiked together through Goblins Forest in the dark, scrambled around boulders at an elevation of 12,760 feet in the early morning, and rested at Boulder Field. The next goal was the Keyhole route (elevation 13,200 feet), which was clearly visible from Boulder Field. When we reached it, we paused at Agnes Vaille Shelter, a structure named for a woman who had died while descending from the first winter ascent of the east face of Longs Peak on January 12, 1925. The east face of Longs includes the Diamond, a sheer granite wall about 1,000 feet in height. It is a world-famous alpine climb requiring skill and strength—the likes of which I do not possess.

The next portion of the hike brought us to the Trough, a wedge in the mountain requiring a vertical climb of 600 feet to reach the Narrows. Somewhere between the Trough, Narrows, and the final part of the ascent, the Homestretch, I remembered to perform a quick self-evaluation and an assessment of Jeremy's physical condition. I knew he could summit, but I wasn't sure about myself. I told Jeremy to go for it. There is only one trail on this part of the mountain, and if I could not summit, I would see him on the way down.

Jeremy made the summit between 12:30 and 1:00 p.m. I joined him about thirty to forty-five minutes later, huffing and puffing all the way. It was exhilarating and satisfying. However, I knew we had to start down in about fifteen minutes. Afternoon thunderstorms are common, and almost every year, at least one climber dies in a fall on the mountain. Experienced mountain climbers understand this. When they speak of their climbing goal, they never say our goal is to reach the summit. They say our goal is to get back down safely. We did. It took about seventeen hours to ascend and get back down. Then we went to Estes Park for vanilla malteds. This was my definition of father-and-child bonding, so I tried the same hike in the summer of 2000 with my daughter, Jessica.

Jessica struggled with alcohol and drugs. I somehow deluded myself into thinking that hiking Longs Peak with her would be spiritu- ally enlightening for us both—maybe even a turning point for Jessica.

It was a tough climb. I tried to follow the plan that had been successful with Jeremy. Estes Park would be our home base for a few day hikes to adjust to the altitude of Rocky Mountain National Park. Then up we'd go. I didn't think I was strong enough to manage the round trip in one day, so we camped overnight at Boulder Field.

That evening, we made dinner using a small stove designed for hikers. It required a bit of warmth to start the flame. One was to keep warm hands on the storage portion of the fuel capsule. Vapors would escape through a valve, and with a match, one could ignite the flame. My hands were too cold. Jessica warmed the capsule, and I lit the flame. We ate dehydrated food—some sort of pasta—and slept in a two-person tent. We began the ascent the next morning.

The weather turned on us. Thunderstorms were visible when we were halfway up the Trough. I estimated we would need sixty to ninety more minutes to summit, but again, the goal was to return safely. I stopped, and Jessica asked what we should do. I hesitated and did not answer. I am sure I looked most pensive. Jessica broke the silence and said I was making this decision for both of us.

At that moment, I knew we had to descend. It was the only safe move. Sometimes I wonder if Jessica saved my life that day. If I had been alone, I would have continued in the storm; instead, we returned safely to California.

Jessica died of a drug overdose on January 22, 2001.

Renaissance Man

Fareed Zakaria wrote a book titled *In Defense of a Liberal Education*. I enjoyed the read, but I didn't need any convincing. I am not sure why I value a liberal education as I do. Perhaps it is all about the values our parents taught us. I vaguely remember thinking (or being told) that education is our most important asset. Unlike freedom or riches, which can be taken away or stolen, knowledge cannot.

Besides, I never thought of college as a vocational school. It was not about preparation for a job. I read a *Braus Blog* post in which the author summarized a key thesis in Zakaria's book: "A college

With our daughter, Jessica, at a photography shop in Estes Park (after much coaxing) following a hike in Rocky Mountain National Park in summer 2000.

Jessica in the 1980s, some of her happiest days.

education is not supposed to prepare you for one job; it is preparation for any job, and for life itself."*

A freshman college student once asked me why there is such a
disproportionate number of Jews who have won Nobel Prizes. I didn't
know about this disproportion. A Wikipedia article begins with this
information: "Nobel Prizes have been awarded to over 900 individuals, of whom at least 20% were Jews, although the Jewish population
comprises less than 0.2% of the world's population. Jews have been
recipients of all six awards."†

---

* "Fareed Zakaria's *In Defense of a Liberal Education*," *Braus Blog*, July 31,
  2018, https://medium.com/braus-blog/fareed-zakarias-in-defense-of-a-liberal
  -education-b20bf8107c69.
† "List of Jewish Nobel Laureates," Wikipedia, last updated April 24, 2021,
  https://en.wikipedia.org/wiki/List_of_Jewish_Nobel_laureates. Dr. Harvey
  Alter, Nobel laureate, has kept the streak alive, winning the award in Physi-
  ology or Medicine in 2020. He taught me about the hepatitis C virus and
  posttransfusion hepatitis at the NIH.

You could make an argument that the search for knowledge is highly valued in Jewish homes. I guess you could also argue that the Royal Swedish Academy of Sciences has a strong positive bias toward Jews. I really cannot explain it, and I am not sure of its importance. All I can say for sure is that I highly value a liberal arts education. When it is achieved, you can say you're a Renaissance man.

The term *Renaissance man* is not meant to omit women. *Merriam-Webster* defines it as "a person who has wide interests and is expert in several areas." That is important, and it is why I was beside myself when I spoke with my son, Jeremy, in 1995.

It was Jeremy's sophomore year at the University of Michigan. He told me he had a job in Ann Arbor, so I no longer needed to support him financially. I didn't interpret this as good news. When I was in college, I found it difficult to hold a job and succeed in class. I chose the latter. For me, it was one or the other, and I said as much to Jeremy.

"Dad, I know that," he said. "That's why I dropped out!"

This was not my concept of a Renaissance man. Perhaps it would be appropriate to say that for the next decade, Jeremy lived the life of a vagabond. This was disconcerting to his Jewish father—and his Catholic mother was not doing so well either.

In the movie *Parenthood*, the character played by Jason Robards explains to the Steve Martin character, "They all grow up, but the worry never ends."

I understand that feeling.

After a while, things changed. Jeremy returned to San Diego and met Danielle while working at the San Diego Natural History Museum. Danielle was like Glinda, the Good Witch of the North. She cast a spell on Jeremy and said, "No college diploma, no marriage."

I understand how dowries work. The bride's family offers goods, money, or an estate to the groom's family. Nonsense. The Delorme family earned the dowry because Danielle brought a special meaning to our entire family. And Jeremy got his degree from San Diego State University.

One day I was with Dorcas Lounsbery and her husband, Ken, bragging about Jeremy graduating from college. Dorcas and Ken are people who make things happen. Many would refer to them as movers and shakers. They shook me up.

I explained that Jeremy was graduating with a major in philosophy and a minor in Latin. He would now be eligible to marry Danielle. Ken turned to me and said, "Jerry, maybe two thousand to three thousand years ago, you could find an advertisement for a philosopher. But you just don't see those ads anymore."

I love Ken's humor, and I still laugh at the line today. But according to Montaigne, my dropout son is the only Renaissance man in the family.

Here is an important section from Sarah Bakewell's book *How to Live, or A Life of Montaigne in One Question and Twenty Attempts at an Answer*:

Command of beautiful and grammatically perfect Latin was the highest goal of a humanistic education: it unlocked the door to the ancient world—considered the locus of all human wisdom—as well as to much of modern culture, since most scholars still wrote Latin. It offered entry to a good career: Latin was essential for legal and civil service. The language bestowed an almost magical blessing on anyone who spoke it. If you spoke well, you must be able to think well. Pierre wanted to give his son the best advantage imaginable: a link both to the lost paradise of antiquity and to a successful personal future.*

Parenthetically, when I was in high school, I was told I needed to study Latin to become a doctor. My high school only taught French and Spanish. Times have changed.

---

* Sarah Bakewell, *How to Live, or A Life of Montaigne in One Question and Twenty Attempts at an Answer* (London: Chatto & Windus, 2011).

Jeremy and his wife, Danielle.

Electric Trains at Christmastime

I really enjoy the Christmas season. I know many people believe "Jesus is the reason for the season," but this just isn't true. People have been celebrating December with lights and presents long before we invented monotheism.

Today, my favorite part of Christmas is the music. But when I was a child, our favorite part of Christmas was having no school for more than a week—and we got presents. Now every fall, I look forward to Dale transforming the living room and sitting with her there with champagne and the season's music.

I am the perfect sucker for John Grisham's book *Skipping Christmas*. He starts out making a fine argument against any effort to string lights around one's house. There is so much unnecessary gift giving and money wasted. And the work of stringing lights violates a key belief I have about life: try not to do work that is designed to be torn apart a few weeks after the task is completed. If I vote against stringing house lights for that reason, you can imagine how I feel about ice carving or sandcastle building!

Yet there are certain expectations one has for the morning of December 25, and few, if any, excuses will be acceptable.

Jeremy was about five or six. And I had a fever of 102 degrees. It was nothing life-threatening, but it was interfering with my ability to concentrate. I was having trouble assembling the electric train set Dale and I bought Jeremy for Christmas.

I worked on the train assembly for over an hour and didn't have the energy to finish. I came up with a plan and shared it with Dale. I told her I needed to go to sleep because I was exhausted and feverish. I would finish setting up the train in the morning. I figured if I completed my task any time on Christmas Day, I would meet the requirement of the holiday season.

Dale looked at me as if I had lobsters coming out of my ears—a line stolen from the 1983 movie *A Christmas Story*. I was told in no uncertain terms that there would be no sleeping in the house until the job was done.

Just like in the book *Skipping Christmas*, we didn't skip Christmas. And the train was set up before sunrise on December 25. Let's face it: that is the way it should be. And Dale made sure of that, thank goodness.

Jeremy, who is forty-four at the time of this writing, and I exchanged a few text messages on December 24, 2020, about the electric train Christmas of decades ago. A few years after that Christmas, sometime

Jeremy and a Z gauge locomotive in 2020.

in the 1980s, I bought the smallest electric train set I had ever seen. Marklin advertised the set with a picture of a walnut that was about twice the size of one of the cars. I hid the set in the closet, believing Jeremy was too young to handle such a small toy. My plan was to protect the set until Jeremy was old enough to enjoy it. The plan failed.

Dale and I downsized from a house to a condominium in July 2017. While packing for the move, I found the Marklin Z gauge train set in a small box. Certainly, Jeremy was old enough to handle this gift, so I gave it to him in 2017 and explained that it had never been opened.

"Not exactly," Jeremy said.

He revealed that he had found the Marklin set shortly after I hid it. He unboxed the trains, set them up, got them to circle on the small tracks, and put them back in the box perfectly so it looked like it was undisturbed all these years.

On Christmas Eve 2020, Jeremy decided to assemble the Z gauge set for old time's sake, but the task was completed on Christmas Day. "That's not allowed," I said. "What happened?"

He said it turned out that his manual dexterity has deteriorated with age, along with any motivation to get the job done before bedtime.

It was the first time I noticed that train sets are a perfect metaphor for that old saying about what goes around, comes around.

Daddy's Home

I never thought of myself as particularly smart, but I also felt one could supplement average to above-average intelligence with "focus, commitment, and sheer will," a line stolen from the movie *John Wick: Chapter 2* starring Keanu Reeves. I have always been persistent and obsessive in my commitments.

Success in medicine required hours of commitment that I knew would be extraordinary. But medicine was and is my dream, so all those lost weekends and missed vacations weren't sacrifices. They were part of the deal.

Yet certain memories haunt me. There was that time when I sat down for dinner with Dale; my son, Jeremy; and my daughter, Jessica. We sat at a round table in the kitchen. I was excited to be with the children because that did not happen often. Just as I sat down, we all heard my beeper. I called the hospital. Dr. Max Savin, one of our excellent surgeons, asked me to return because he needed confirmation that the vagus nerve he intentionally severed was indeed nerve tissue. In the early 1980s, surgeons cut the vagus nerve to treat peptic ulcers. Now we use medicine. I remember being conflicted. I wanted an evening with the family. But I had a responsibility to the patient and the surgeon. Of course, I returned to the hospital. When I got home, everyone was asleep.

Another memory is a day I came home from the hospital, pulled the car into the garage, entered the house somewhat exhausted, and heard three-year-old Jessica say, "Daddy's home! Daddy's home! Daddy's home!" I got three "Daddy's home" exclamations in rapid succession. I felt wanted. I felt needed. I had redeeming value. It was one of the happiest days of my life.

Maybe I just don't know how to be efficient at work. PMC had a cardiac surgeon, Rob Reichman, who was superb at his craft but in his "free time" flew an airplane. I asked Rob how he had time to be a cardiac surgeon and fly an airplane. He answered me with a joke that basically explained that there are few things more foolish than a physician who thinks he can excel at his profession and also be a good pilot. I cannot speak to Rob's piloting skills, but he was great in the operating room.

Another doctor told me you could not be good at medicine if you are good at anything else. "If you show me a doctor who is good at golf," he said, "I will show you an incompetent doctor." That's a little exaggeration to make a point. This work of medicine is really tough.

I was not home often. This is probably surprising to many who don't understand the life of a pathologist. Nonetheless, my absence from the family disturbed me.

There was one time when I came home and Jessica asked if we could get a dog. I said no. Jessica really wanted a dog. I got her a goldfish. I would come home from work and check how the fish was doing. For several days in a row, when I checked on the fish, the water was murky. I asked Jessica why the water was so dirty. Jessica said her fish had asked her to pet him.

My mom had a German shepherd when she was growing up in an apartment in the Bronx, but she told me not to get a dog. I remember asking her why. "Children grow up; dogs do not," she said.

After a while, Jessica came back with a new approach to her plan. "When Daddy dies," she asked Mom, "can we get a dog?" Mom said yes.

The Ladder

We blame others when events occur that we believe should not have happened. Often the reason for blaming others is the fact that it is too painful to blame the responsible party—ourselves. But sometimes we believe someone else is accountable for an event we cannot explain.

For years we had a housekeeper, Wendy, who did a miraculous job of keeping the house in order. But periodically, something I needed urgently was not in the location where I had last placed it. I would come home from work and blame Wendy. She worked for us for over ten years. I should be ashamed of the number of times I blamed her for moving an object that I could not find.

Dale and I came home late one evening in the 1990s from an event on a school night. From the driveway, I saw a stepladder outside Jeremy's window. We checked on the kids. Jeremy was not in his bed, and his bedroom window was wide open. This was disturbing because we live by the beach and had been burglarized since we moved into the house in 1978.

How careless of Wendy to leave the window open! It was an invitation to the street people. And the stepladder beckoned the intruder to please come right in and take what they wanted.

I called Dale into the room as my witness: "Dale, note the window was carelessly left open by our housekeeper, Wendy. Can you believe she cleaned the windows and then left the stepladder outside with the window opened? Amazing!" I proceeded to retrieve the stepladder and close the window.

Dale paused for a moment. What happened next reminds me of a scene from *Moonstruck* when Cher slaps Nicolas Cage in the face. Cher yells, "Snap out of it!"

Dale pointed out with a little irritation, "Wendy does not clean our windows. She never cleans the windows. You are looking at evidence provided by your son."

He had escaped from his bedroom window. The stepladder was part of his plan to reenter the house. This possibility was beyond my comprehension. Why would my son leave through the window? We have a front door.

"What's the matter with you?" Dale asked. "Jeremy didn't want us to know he was gone."

Did you ever see the movie *The Birdcage* with Robin Williams and Gene Hackman? Robin Williams plays a gay guy living with his love, played by Nathan Lane. The character of Gene Hackman's wife, played by Dianne Wiest, tries to explain to him that the couple is gay.

She tells her husband that these two men love each other. He cannot comprehend this concept. His disbelief matches my lack of understanding as to why Jeremy would go out the window, leaving the stepladder evidence behind. I clung to my position that Wendy was to blame. Dale said something like "Get real."

I am teachable. I decided to consider Dale's theory of the stepladder event. I armed the security system so it would trigger if the front door was opened. It triggered late that night. I caught the perpetrator. It was my son.

It eventually dawned on me that further discussion on this matter would be appropriate. I asked Jeremy directly if he had tried to escape from his own house through the window and then left a stepladder outside as evidence that he did the deed.

"Yes," he said.

"Are you sure this isn't Wendy's fault?" I queried.

"Dad, I did it," he said.

"But why?"

"I didn't want you to know I was going out on a school night. You would not have permitted it. So I just did it."

My last question: "Well, why would you leave evidence of this misdeed?"

"I didn't think this was evidence," Jeremy said. He saw it as a way to get back into his bedroom.

Sometimes the world does not match the way we put the pieces together. "Things are not always as they seem" is a quotation attributed to Phaedrus of Plato's time.

In deciding how to live one's life, it is best not to play the victim. Events are not always thrust upon you. You may have had a hand in ensuring their occurrence.

Poky and His Struggles in the Real World

Sometime in the late 1970s or early 1980s, we read *The Poky Little Puppy* to our kids. The children's book was written by Janette Sebring Lowrey and illustrated by Gustaf Tenggren and first published in 1942.

According to Wikipedia, it is the best-selling hardcover children's book of all time in the United States. With about 15 million copies sold, it exceeds the sales of Dr. Seuss's *Green Eggs and Ham*.

I acquired the name Poky Puppy in my thirties because the environment easily distracted me, just like the poky puppy. I certainly was more pensive than active. Outside of the workplace, I tended to be less aware of my surroundings.

I am slower to perform manual tasks than many; recall my lack of speed in the operating room, which I described earlier in this book. Yet there is more to my story than just the lack of physical speed. There is a certain slowness to comprehension. If there is more than one way of looking at a situation, I tend to choose the interpretation that is not embraced by others.

Someone looks at the beach and opines that the tide is out. My mind gets confused by a sentence like that. Most people would interpret the sentence to mean that it's low tide—that is, the rise and fall of the sea that happens twice each day is now low. So more beach is visible. Most refer to this as the tide being "out." I struggle with it. I consider the tide a portion of the sea "moving out" to the beach. If a portion of the sea is out, I reason incorrectly, there is less beach. We need to wait until the tide goes back into the ocean from whence it came. Get that tide back into the sea so we can play beach volleyball.

Now do you see why Dale wonders how I function in the real world?

In my Walter Mitty–like life, I often think of the movie *The Count of Monte Cristo* and the line delivered by the chief magistrate, J. F. Villefort, to Edmond Dantes: "Foolish and innocent. I believe these are the worst charges that can be leveled against you . . . God knows how you're going to survive in this world, Edmond Dantes."

Such bizarre thinking as illustrated previously regarding the tide happens to me in other common situations. I approach an elevator bank and see two buttons outside the doors. An "Up" button and a "Down" button. I am on the eighth floor and want to go to the lobby. At the top of the elevator doors, I can see the current location of the elevator. It's on the second floor, so I push the "Up" button. Why would I do this when I want to go to the lobby? Because my brain is telling me what the elevator needs to do next, which is get up here. When it arrives, I will tell it to go down to the lobby.

With that as background, you can imagine how courageous Dale was in the early 1980s when she announced she was leaving town for a couple of days to give a talk in Honolulu. Perhaps Dale's reason for doing this was akin to the concept of tossing me into the pool to learn to swim. Leaving me with the two kids at home, Jessica around four and Jeremy about seven, seemed like high-risk behavior.

I wasn't worried about Jeremy. He was raising me, as I have mentioned. But Jessica was in preschool. Dale always brought her to Gillispie School looking so cute, with her hair in pigtails just like Cindy Lou Who in Dr. Seuss's *How the Grinch Stole Christmas.*

As I explained in "My Kingdom for a Procedure Manual," my plan was to improvise an approach to successfully complete my two- to three-day assignment.

"How about putting Jessica's hair in pigtails just before you leave for the airport?" I suggested. "Then her hair would always be ready for the day's activities."

Dale blurted out that I was not putting our daughter to bed for two nights in pigtails. Dale could not believe such foolishness. But it got worse.

When it was time to dress Jessica for preschool, I took the panties out of the drawer and quickly put them on her. Just like with the tide and the elevator, I reasoned incorrectly: No external genitalia, so it doesn't matter how you put those panties on as long as you don't put both legs in the same opening. Wrong! It is possible to put panties on incorrectly. And I did.

Upon Dale's return, I had a memorable feeling of relief when I was no longer forced to perform a task without proficiency training. I also had to endure the embarrassing assessment of one of the parents of another Gillispie student.

"So you were out of town for a few days," she said to Dale.

"How did you know that?" Dale asked.

"You should have seen how Jessica was dressed!" came the reply.

I should add that my sense of design is nonexistent. When I went to meetings alone in the 1980s, Dale put sticky notes on my shirts and ties so I would properly match the pair and thereby reflect well on her design reputation.

I guess Dale was right. I just couldn't function in the real world. Thank goodness I could deliver in surgical pathology and blood banking.

Learning the Creative Use of Money

I am certainly a creature of habit. I get set in my ways, and only stress, physical or mental, will motivate me to deviate from an established course. For example, when I was in high school, we took public transportation to reach the campus. We were too young to drive and certainly could not afford a taxi. There were just two choices: take the Q25/Q34 bus on Parsons Boulevard to Jamaica High School or walk. I took the bus. It was habit. And it was cheap.

In 1962, the bus ride cost fifteen cents, but students got a discount pass. I was proud to live within my limited budget, which was an allowance of five dollars a week. Today, the same ride is $2.75.

Of course, that's not the only thing that costs more today. Did you know that the Motel 6 chain, founded in 1962, got its name by charging six dollars a night for a room? Those who ran the chain believed six bucks was enough to cover building costs, land leases, and janitorial supplies. As time moved on, the name remained Motel 6, although six dollars would not be enough for the sales tax on an average room today. The 1960s were a time of cost control, and I learned the value of money.

This all changed sometime after college. I started to enjoy the finer things that money could buy. Usually, I was introduced to the power of the dollar by an event paid for by my employer. For example, during our residency days, we were encouraged to attend professional meetings that often were held in exciting locations, such as our nation's capital—or perhaps a rare West Coast seminar. I stayed in huge hotels and did something I never imagined. You could hang a card on your doorknob at night, and the next morning, your breakfast would be delivered to your room!

These little pleasures were just the beginning. It took Dale to bring me to the next level.

In 1983, the American Association of Blood Banks, now simply called the AABB, met in New York City. We had discovered the American Airlines frequent-flier program, which is one of the first programs that made flying first-class seemingly inexpensive if you had the miles to cover the journey. So off to NYC, my first time in about ten years, in first class. That was the beginning of the transformation. Dale opined that it was the only way to travel. She was just warming up.

I remember on a trip to NYC, again first class, Dale said a taxi did not provide comfort equal to that of our first-class seats. My imagination was too limited. Really, is there a more comfortable way to get from the airport to the hotel than a taxi? Certainly it beats the bus, shuttle, or rental car. Dale offered another option: How about a limousine? I hadn't known there were limos and comfortable sedans that we could take from the airport to our hotel. I tried it. That's all it took.

Of course, all this costs money. I spend a lot. I will never be accused of living life according to an austerity plan, though I often wonder what that would look like. I have decided austerity is a good thing when one's financial condition requires it. Fortunately, my financial condition was made secure by my dad. It took him four years to convince me to save, but when he got the savings plan in motion, we bought a thirty-year, zero-coupon treasury bond for $20,000 at about 12 percent interest. That was in 1981. In 2011, the bond paid $1,280,000.

Dale's teachings proved their value yet again on a trip we took to Houston, where we visited Dale's mom and dad, Jean and Donald Monday. That weekend visit occurred during an unbelievable rainstorm that flooded the Avis parking lot and made it impassable. When it finally dawned on me that we were not leaving the immediate vicinity of the airport that night, I hoped we could spend the night at an airport hotel.

This again illustrates my naïveté. Being poky when it comes to any action, I arrived with Dale at the hotel after a long line of passengers had already formed to seek a room for the night. This looked hopeless. I sat in the corner, envisioning a poor night's sleep in the lobby lounge. After all, not only were we stranded at the airport; employees who worked at the hotel could not reach their place of work. Housekeeping was seriously compromised. Also, there were employees who couldn't leave work. They did double duty trying to get rooms ready for the onslaught of crabby passengers lined up in the lobby and doing some first-class complaining. This was when Dale's ingenuity saved the day.

We were last in line for a room in the hotel. But Dale didn't want a room. She went up to the counter and inquired, "Do you have any suites?" The woman on the other side of the counter said suites were available, but they cost more than twice that of a room. The receptionist offered that no one had reserved a suite recently, so a suite could be immediately occupied. Dale sealed the deal without even discussing it with me. She came over and just said that the poky husband married the perfect wife and that we would sleep comfortably. And we did.

Food delivery trucks could not reach the hotel that night. The restaurant only served spaghetti, but it had California wine. Turns out you can live on either bread and wine or spaghetti and wine. We chose the latter.

Mom, When Are You Leaving Town Again?

It was the late 1980s. Jessica was at sleep-away summer camp. Jeremy and I were home alone for a few days because Dale had gone to visit her dad in a Houston hospital. Jeremy was about ten, and he was fun to take to dinner. We had a three-day weekend.

On Friday night, we dined at Maitre D', a restaurant in which Jeremy would one day work as a busboy. For La Jolla dining, this restaurant was special. Tony Curtis and his young date once sat across from us, so the restaurant's reputation had reached the Hollywood market.

This was valuable time with Jeremy because my work schedule too often kept me away from the family. Jeremy was young, but he behaved like an adult in the fine restaurants we explored. For me, these were serene moments. What more could I ask for? Father and son, quiet restaurant, and white linen tablecloths. For Jeremy, I suspect it was an adventure, by which I mean "explorer-like." For dinner at Maitre D', Jeremy chose the alligator for his main course.

This was no austerity weekend. After Maitre D' on Friday night, it was Mr. A's on Saturday night. Back in the 1980s, Mr. A's was all about the view. The cuisine was just OK until Bertrand Hug took over the place in 2000 and renamed it Bertrand's at Mr. A's. His French education, training, and experience (he was born in rural southwestern France and studied economics at the University of Toulouse) paid off in San Diego and in Rancho Santa Fe, where he owns Mille Fleurs, an elegant French restaurant. Both of these restaurants today are superb and represent some of the finest dining in San Diego County.

Then there was Elario's on La Jolla Shores Drive, less than a half-mile from our house on Vallecitos. Again, I went for the view. Edward O. Wilson wrote in *The Meaning of Human Existence* that humans feel safe and more at ease when we view our surroundings from an elevated position. From a Darwinian point of view, elevation increases your chance of survival. You have a better opportunity to detect predators when you are looking down on the savanna.

This three-day weekend was not just about exceptional cuisine. I was a student of Kenpo Karate at the Twin Dragons dojo. Terry Wade Sanchez is still the owner and is a sixth-degree black belt. I learned that Terry, on occasion, practiced his shooting skills at a gun range near the airport, and on Saturday of our special weekend, Jeremy, Terry, and I shot pistols at the range. At first, I shot a .22-caliber gun. But then I saw my first .357 Magnum, and Terry said, "Go ahead. Shoot that pistol."

The .357 Magnum is heavy, and I had difficulty handling the recoil. I went back to the .22 for target practice. Jeremy also shot the .22-caliber gun. Then on Sunday, Dale returned from Houston. We walked into the airport and headed directly for the gate, which you could still do in 1986. I gave Dale a kiss. Jeremy didn't. He had a question: "Mom, when are you going out of town again?" This was not the welcome Dale was hoping for, but we can laugh about it now.

EIGHT

Professional Career

Climate Change

During the winter, schools in New York City sometimes closed due to excessive snow accumulation that made it impossible (or at least very difficult) for public transportation to bring kids to school. Any snow day was an exciting happening for a high school student. Of course, until I left New York at age seventeen, I didn't know of any other life. We enjoyed four seasons. Winter was the worst, and the other three were great.

In college in Ann Arbor, Michigan, and in medical school in Detroit, the winter was more challenging than in NYC. I remember that the digital thermometer over the Ann Arbor Bank often showed a minus sign. The minus degree visual was often accompanied by wind—not like Chicago but still bone-chilling. It all reminded me of the poem by Robert W. Service titled "The Cremation of Sam McGee":

There are strange things done in the midnight sun
By the men who moil for gold;
The Arctic trails have their secret tales
That would make your blood run cold;
The Northern Lights have seen queer sights,
But the queerest they ever did see
Was that night on the marge of Lake Lebarge
I cremated Sam McGee.

Sam is cremated after he freezes to death in the Arctic. But what is queer about that? Well, Sam is placed in the furnace, and though he is dead, he sits up, and the narrator of the poem says,

> And there sat Sam, looking cool and calm, in the heart of the
> furnace roar;
> And he wore a smile you could see a mile, and he said:
> "Please close that door.
> It's fine in here, but I greatly fear you'll let in the cold and
> storm—
> Since I left Plumtree, down in Tennessee, it's the first time
> I've been warm."*

For me, Michigan was cold and, in many ways, lonely. Arthur Miller, playwright and a graduate of the university, wrote, "My first affection for the University of Michigan was due, simply, to their accepting me."† He also wrote an essay about a return visit to his alma mater. He described an intangible coldness in the atmosphere. He wasn't just talking about climate.

Yet I remember a group of senior medical students encouraging me to intern at Detroit Receiving Hospital. We could stick together and make Detroit "a great place to live," the reasoning went. This had a romantic component that appealed to my idealism, but I was worried about weather that could make a day in Antarctica feel temperate. Dale and I sailed across the Drake Passage from Ushuaia, Argentina, to Antarctica, on January 5, 2001, stepping off the *Prince Albert II* onto the coldest continent on the planet. January is Antarctica's summer, but it was still Antarctica. I remember saying to Dale, "Finally no hot flashes for you." But the truth be known, the Antarctic Peninsula in January cannot compete with Detroit in winter. Did I really want to stay and make Detroit a great place to live?

---

* Robert W. Service, "The Cremation of Sam McGee," in *Songs of a Sourdough* (Edward Stern, 1907).
† Fredric Alan Maxwell, "Arthur Miller's Ode to U-M," Michigan Today, November 25, 2013, http://michigantoday.umich.edu/arthur-millers-ode-to-u-m/.

I may have been idealistic, but the pragmatic in me took over. I thought Detroit could not be made a great place to live in my lifetime. This was not an excuse to exit the cold and gray of Michigan. If a position had been offered to me in Ann Arbor, I would have endured the cold and gray. Detroit was just filled with too much hate to be made great in one person's lifetime.

I read an advertisement in the Sunday edition of the *Detroit Free Press* in the winter of 1968. There was a picture of water rimmed by palm trees. The caption read, "Some people go on vacation, other people live there." I wanted to live there.

I left for an internship and residency in Boston. This is called jumping from the frying pan into the fire. In an earlier essay, "The Spleen," I explained why Boston was the "fire." Let's just call it fire and ice. Boston's winters were as tough as Michigan's. Then came Bethesda, Maryland. Bethesda was the opposite of Boston. The culture of the National Institutes of Health (NIH) was one of respect and patience. At Massachusetts General Hospital (MGH), there was the tendency to elevate oneself by simultaneously performing at a stratospheric level and assuring others that they were not worthy of MGH.

I loved NIH. That was the climate change I was looking for. NIH was just like Ann Arbor but for adults only! I was offered a job as head of surgical pathology but as a civil servant—not as a commissioned officer in the Public Health Service. The benefits of being head of surgical pathology and a captain in the Public Health Service are great, and I wanted all that. I got the job but without the commission. I left for La Jolla.

James A. Michener, the Pulitzer Prize–winning author, wrote the novel *Hawaii* in 1959. He explained that the natives of Tahiti who were pushed out and sailed to establish Hawaii had been vanquished. That is just how I felt when I left the NIH for my first job in California as a surgical pathologist at Palomar and Pomerado hospitals in San Diego County. I chose to live in La Jolla, a thirty-five-minute drive to work.

La Jolla's average temperature is around seventy degrees. It never snows, but you can ski if you drive two or three hours to Big Bear. You can also snorkel and scuba dive if you drive about five minutes.

The place is surrounded by palm trees. For a native of New York City, this place was a real-life Disneyland. I called Bethesda an Ann Arbor for adults only. La Jolla is Ann Arbor for rich adults only. I didn't think I would fit in, but I was going to try.

In my first three years in La Jolla, I was homesick for Ann Arbor. I tried to talk my way into a job at St. Joseph's Mercy Hospital there, but they had no position for a pathologist. I didn't care. I asked for an interview and argued that the pathology group should take advantage of me. "Pay me intern wages," I argued. "But if a position opens in the next few years, you will know what a good decision you made today." The answer was no. I was forced to stay in La Jolla.

I still miss Bethesda. I sometimes wonder how my life would have changed if I had gotten the commission in the Public Health Service. When I wonder about it, I come to two conclusions: I would have struggled at the NIH, and I would not be rich and in La Jolla.

I have adjusted to the climate change. I guess John Lennon was right when he said, "Life is what happens while you are busy making other plans."*

A Pathologist's Bedside Manner

I joined the medical staffs of Palomar Medical Center (PMC) and Pomerado Hospital in 1977. These hospitals are now part of Palomar Health, a public entity in North San Diego County. After practicing surgical pathology at these facilities from 1977 to 1988, I established a community blood bank for Palomar Health.

At first, my principal responsibility was to collect whole blood from volunteer donors, test the blood for safety, and prepare blood components for transfusion. We delivered blood to our hospitals and other hospitals in San Diego County and sometimes points farther north. Eventually, we expanded to apheresis.

---

* An internet search indicates that the line was first attributed to Allen Saunders in a January 1957 *Reader's Digest* magazine as "Life is what happens to us while we are making other plans."

Apheresis is a word derived from Greek meaning "taking away." In blood banking, it is an automated process of removing whole blood from a vein and then spinning it in a centrifuge so that separation occurs among the red blood cells, platelets, and plasma. The process can be used to collect these individual blood components and prepare them for transfusion. You can also use the same equipment to treat patients with selected diseases. One such patient was a mom who had a near fatal disease that was successfully treated with apheresis, specifically plasma exchange.

Mom was flown from a desert town by helicopter to PMC after her husband found her unconscious on the floor of their home. She had seizures and needed to be intubated. Upon arrival in the Emergency Department, it was quickly recognized that the patient had a rare condition called thrombotic thrombocytopenic purpura. Let's call it TTP. Patients with this condition can become critically ill with anemia, low platelet count, neurologic abnormalities, fever, and kidney failure. TTP is a medical emergency and requires immediate plasma exchange.

The unconscious mom could return to good health if we could remove her plasma and replace it with normal plasma from healthy blood donors. If we moved fast enough, we could bring a patient back to good health 90 percent of the time. There was reason to be optimistic, though you can understand why this was not the husband's state of mind. The daughter had not been contacted yet. She was in the San Francisco Bay Area.

I explained the treatment plan to the husband. I said it would take about forty-eight hours, sometimes less, to know if the treatment was effective. I'm a pathologist. The reputation of pathologists was best described by an internist friend of mine who said he has never met a pathologist who wasn't already dead. We are not known for our bedside manner. Yet I bonded with the husband and spent considerable time with him during his wife's hospitalization.

On the second day of hospitalization, the pulmonologist removed the breathing tube. Mom was awake but not talking. When I walked into the room on day three, mom was sitting up in bed and chatting with her husband. I got a great smile from the guy. Not surprisingly, the patient did not know who I was. I told the same story to mom as I told the husband. Everyone was comfortable with the treatment plan. The clinical improvement was so dramatic, it could have been described as a modern-day miracle.

When I left the hospital that day, I thought about what a tremendous high I was experiencing. To be able to help people who really appreciate the health care team's work is a blessing. That is not always the case. Nurses and doctors are often attacked by unruly patients, albeit most of these patients have behavioral health issues. Nonetheless, I went home loving my work—until the next day.

When I walked into the room on day four, everything was great. Mom had put on lipstick. Her husband greeted me with a big smile. I promptly said that I could not imagine things going any better. The daughter disagreed. She looked me in the eye and said, "You call this good? My mother lost her memory!" The daughter's perception caught me off guard. I was not able to detect a loss of memory, but a complete return of brain function could take more than a few days. I wasn't worried, but the daughter was angry.

I am not sure what my body language said about me at the time. Remember, I am a pathologist. I had not yet taken any courses in self-awareness. I suspect my body language was interpreted as dismissive. In truth, I was not buying into any cerebral compromise on day four. "You don't believe me," the daughter said to me after approaching rapidly. "I am telling you there is something wrong with my mother."

She asked me to watch, turned toward Mom, and said, "Name your five cats." My patient had no trouble naming the first three cats, but she could go no further. I saw the frustration on the patient's face. She tried again, but cat number three was a far as her memory would permit. "Do you see what I am talking about? Do you see this?" the daughter said. "Just what are you going to do about it?"

My response was what I call high-risk behavior. I knew what I was doing. I was relying on my relationship with the husband. I turned toward the daughter, looked briefly at her mom, and said with an air of confidence, "Your mother has too many cats."

The daughter reported me to the chief medical officer (CMO), but so did her father, who provided a glowing description of his wife's treatment and made a sizable donation to the hospital's philanthropic foundation. I never spoke with the daughter again. I like to believe that the family jokes about that insensitive New York doctor who was part of the team that brought mom back to them.

The Bow Tie

I wear a bow tie. Some people think it is a statement. Bow ties are associated with geeks, though recent evidence has shown that the appeal may be broader in scope. Bow tie manufacturers, companies that make millions of these a year, sell the "pre-tied" style the most. According to internet sites, as many as 78 percent of all bow ties manufactured are "pre-tied." That makes sense because only 1 percent of men know how to tie a bow tie.

Bow ties are not only worn by geeks; they are the tie of choice for formal occasions. Not surprisingly, New Year's Eve is the day of the most internet hits on sites that show how to tie the knot. Winning the silver and bronze award for internet hits are Christmas and Halloween, respectively.

For about forty years, I've been wearing bow ties, but when I first started wearing them, I had no message to convey. An article published in the medical journal *Lancet* provided evidence that physicians who wore long neckties had a greater chance of spreading germs to patients than those who wore bow ties. My interest in quality and safety led some health care workers to believe there was a method to my madness. This was not the case.

In the early 1980s, Dr. Jim Bulen, a surgeon at PMC Escondido, was performing a thyroidectomy. The patient had a nodule in the thyroid, and Dr. Bulen wanted to know if the nodule was malignant. That's what surgical pathologists do for a living—tell you if something is benign or malignant. Jim brought me the bloody organ in his bare hands. It was the 1980s, and today, that would be an educational "infection control" moment for the surgeon. I suggested (but did not demand) he wear gloves. By the way, the gloves were latex.

The next case was a left breast biopsy handed to me directly by Dr. Edward Greer. He meticulously pointed out the suspicious area and asked me to observe carefully and freeze that exact site. I leaned over to look, and as I did, my long necktie swiped against the breast biopsy. I proceeded with the task at hand. But that tie was stained. I'm obsessive-compulsive about these things and don't think a guy should wear a stained tie, which is interesting because history tells us that the purpose of long neckties was to protect the costly shirt from being stained. Over time, the tie became as expensive as the shirt!

When I got home, I could smell the croutons from the kitchen. The aroma of garlic and olive oil could only mean a Caesar salad—my all-time-favorite dinner. I opened a bottle of Silver Oak cabernet and sat down to enjoy the salad and wine—no second course needed or desired. This is called a perfect ending to a stressful day.

After I poured Dale a glass of wine, she looked at my tie and asked what the stain was.

"Left breast," I said.

Dale was appalled and tossed out all my long neckties. The next day, I had a choice of a half dozen bow ties.

The Hemoglobin Is Significantly Elevated

Larry Macklin was the supervisor of the hematology section of the clinical laboratory at PMC Escondido in 1977. Dr. Alfred Musgrave was one of the pathologists working in the lab with me. These two gentlemen provided me great entertainment during my first few years in private practice at Palomar.

Larry had a sense of humor, and he knew hematology. He was also one of the few people I met who not only enjoyed calligraphy but demonstrated significant talent with the art form. One day he mentioned that I had to join Dr. Musgrave when he made early morning rounds in the laboratory. Dr. Musgrave was a very good surgical pathologist, but I was not familiar with his interest in the clinical lab. So I joined him.

These early morning rounds were not at all like I expected. Dr. Musgrave lectured the medical technologists on the importance of saving for their future. I strongly believed in sound financial planning, but I

My bow tie is not a fashion statement. It's very practical. Photo courtesy of Dr. George Kung.

didn't see it as part of the pathologist's job description. I was unprepared for what happened next. Dr. Musgrave started giving advice to the technologists as if he were their personal financial advisor.

He told them to buy gold. He tried to explain that gold was the only safe bet for their future. This bothered me quite a bit, but not as much as it did Larry Macklin. Larry explained to me in private that most medical technologists are in no position to buy South African Krugerrands (gold coins), especially in the magnitude Dr. Musgrave was advocating. Furthermore, he was distracting the staff from their morning run, their busiest time of day. Larry told me it was my responsibility to stop this interference.

I didn't act on the day Larry gave me that assignment, but I engaged when I heard Dr. Musgrave raising his voice in an air of reprimand directed to Larry. Basically, Dr. Musgrave had lost confidence in the hematology section's ability to perform a simple lab test, the complete blood count. "Look at this," screamed Musgrave. "Just two hours ago, this patient's hemoglobin was five grams per deciliter. Now you are telling me it almost doubled to nine grams. Just what do you expect me to do?"

"Sell!" Larry replied.

Larry knew the patient had just been transfused, but Musgrave didn't. And Larry knew I hadn't spoken to Dr. Musgrave. This is how Larry motivated me to proceed with an intervention. That was the last we all heard about the Krugerrand.

Dorothy Farrow (1928–2019)

Just a few months after my thirtieth birthday, I completed my residency and fellowship in clinical pathology and blood banking at the NIH. It was time to look for employment. I found a position as a surgical pathologist at Palomar Health. In 1977, it was called Palomar Hospital and Pomerado Hospital, the two acute care facilities comprising the Northern San Diego County Hospital District, a public entity. I began my first job earning $60,000 per year. This represented a huge jump in pay from $10,000 per year as an intern at MGH and about $20,000 per year as a resident at the NIH.

I hadn't been exposed to the basic principles of management or budgeting during training. I was good at what I did, but I did not realize I was wasteful. The lab manager was tracking the use of supplies, specifically latex gloves. Yes, in 1977, the only gloves in the operating rooms and labs were latex. We didn't know any better. And I didn't know how fast I went through them. I used more than any other pathologist. None of us thought about the savings we would enjoy by using the same nonsterile product.

The lab manager addressed the issue in an unusual way. He came to me and said, "Dr. Kolins, this is the last latex glove you will have today. You will need to use the same pair all day while you cut the surgical specimens. We won't be getting any more gloves today."

The focus on budget and expense was not something I recognized as important. It wasn't until 1994, when I earned a master of arts degree in organizational management, that I was required to pass a class called Profit Planning and Control, but my first class in the subject was an involuntary encounter with Dorothy Farrow, RN, the manager of the operating rooms at Palomar Hospital.

I ignored the direction I had received from the lab manager and went around the corner to the operating room and asked a nurse for one pair of latex gloves. She handed me the gloves. Dorothy watched. I left for the surgical cutting bench. The same thing happened the next day. The lab manager allotted me one pair of gloves for my day's work; in the afternoon, I returned to the OR for my second pair. Dorothy stepped forward and said, "Please join me in my office for a minute. I want to show you something."

I was young, excited about my work, and had brought a New York City ego to Escondido. Also, most of the OR staff were aware of my recent consultation in which I provided our prominent surgeon, Dr. Bernard Graybill, with an unanticipated diagnosis that saved his patient from an unnecessary procedure. With a start like that, I thought Dorothy was going to commend me on my superb performance.

Dorothy pulled out a "green bar" report. It was a term we used because green and white horizontal lines alternated on a spreadsheet, making each line easier to read. One of the lines was labeled "Supplies." Dorothy pointed to it and asked me to look at the amount of money budgeted for OR supplies. Then she pointed to the column that showed how much she spent. Dorothy spent about the amount she was budgeted to spend, maybe a bit less. She asked if I wanted to make her look bad.

I felt terrible. Dorothy was easy to like and fun to talk to. It never occurred to me that my afternoon visits to the OR could have a detrimental effect on her performance review, and I apologized. I never went back to the OR to ask for gloves, but I was convinced there was a gap in my education. I started to pay attention to actions of mine that caused others to report overtime. I stopped using sterile gloves and told the other pathologists we all needed to use nonsterile gloves. Eventually, I started to see opportunities all over the place to save money.

Someone very close to me once said, "You are the only person I know who could exceed an unlimited budget." Dorothy was the catalyst who straightened me out. And I aced the final in Profit Planning and Control.

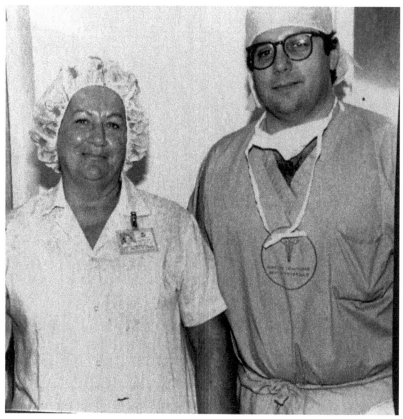

Dorothy Farrow, RN, director of operating rooms, and Dr. Rob Reichman, cardiac surgeon (and private pilot), in the 1980s.

I'm Seventy-One

As the chief quality officer (CQO) of Palomar Health reporting to the CEO, I was invited to a Nashville conference called What's Right with Healthcare, which provided a good introduction to quality and safety for the Palomar system's new CEO, CMO, and COO. These talented individuals had never held such positions in the past. And at the August 2018 conference, they got to hear speakers from Baldrige Award–winning health systems talk about their journeys.

Diane Hansen, the newly appointed CEO, had been promoted to the job from CFO. Diane, to my surprise, enjoyed a good party. Each night she took the four of us and the chief nursing officer,

Larry LaBossiere, to a nightclub with the best music Nashville had to offer and plenty of drinks. I'd had my seventy-first birthday on April 2, and it was not easy keeping up with these forty- and fifty-year-olds. I must have looked exhausted one night because Diane told me that it was OK to go back to the hotel early. I took her up on this offer.

One night we went to a place called Ole Red at 300 Broadway, Nashville. Ole Red described itself as "always itching to have a little fun with food, drink, and music that raises the bar on Broadway." Diane was dancing alone with her drink in hand, really into the Nashville scene. I was still recovering from a ruptured L4-5 right foraminal disc injury that had occurred on July 7, 2018. I still carried my Xtreme Comforts seat cushion to help ensure complete healing.

Imagine this scene. Dozens of people on the dance floor and me walking in holding a cushion designed for those with back injuries. I was standing and just watching the scene, holding my cushion, when a young lady came over to me and started a conversation. I was surprised how comfortably and physically close she stood while asking questions about the cushion. I told her of my injury and explained that the cushion was a turning point. I was now off all medications and just holding my security cushion tight. She told me she thought she could use one and pursued the conversation.

It occurred to me that there was a small possibility that her approach wasn't simply about the cushion, but any such notion seemed ridiculous. We spoke for a few minutes. Then a guy came over and asked me what I was doing. I must have looked puzzled because that's the way I felt.

He accused me of messing with his fiancée, and he didn't like it. "What do you have to say about that?" he said with menace.

All I could think of to say was, "I'm seventy-one."

The following photograph suggests that my comment did not assuage his anxiety. I just don't think that marriage will work.

The author is being warned to keep his distance from the gentleman's fiancée. I still believe the warning was unnecessary. I had already told him I was seventy-one.

Cleaning House

I have worked at Palomar Health in various positions since Labor Day, 1977. For more than a decade, surgical pathology was all-consuming, yet the most exciting years were spent in hospital administration. I had no formal training in this field; I just gravitated toward it. On January 23, 2018, the new CEO of Palomar Health named me CQO, reporting directly to the CEO. It was the height of my career, and it didn't last long.

Other changes occurred that January. Of the sixteen leaders in our organization, seven were laid off along with thirty-five folks in marketing, information technology, organizational learning, and revenue cycle. During my first meeting with the new executive team, I decided to say something risky. When I saw the organizational chart and the forty-two empty boxes representing the players who were no longer with us, I said, "The CEO eliminated the heads of the Five Families. This day would make Michael Corleone jealous."

The chief HR officer smiled. My risk was rewarded with acceptance. The acceptance lasted almost one full year.

Being the CQO was the most fun I ever had in a job. I should add that fun is determined by many factors in one's life. It is easier to have fun at work when you feel financially secure. At the age of thirty-five with a dependent family and with job performance determined by style, content, and outcome, work was the opposite of fun. Not meeting job expectations could have devastating effects on one's health, both physical and emotional. Holding an insecure administrative position (which is the definition of all health care administrative positions) at thirty-five would have been fraught with anxiety—not fun. There is another thing about being financially secure: I'm less inhibited. That is not necessarily a good thing.

At the beginning of my time as the CQO, I had several naïve moments. My emotional nonintelligence (that sounds kinder than emotional stupidity) caused me to believe that chiefs who reported to the CEO were fully responsible for their sections. I could not conceive of the influence various executives had over the CEO in areas remote from their expertise.

Here is my favorite example of emotional stupidity for which I must accept full responsibility. The CEO apparently recognized that the COO needed help and decided to award the management of the operating rooms and the perioperative platform to the CMO. This was a system-wide operations position and an excellent opportunity for an inexperienced CMO to show his stuff. But the COO did not immediately embrace the decision. After the CEO announced that the administrative change was immediate, the COO explained that a change in the reporting structure could not occur until the next day.

The COO was determined to assess the degree to which the operating room personnel would accept the new line of authority.

I was comfortable with my next comments. After all, I had read Thomas J. Peters's book *In Search of Excellence: Lessons from America's Best-Run Companies*. As I spoke to the executive team, I was living the one paragraph from the book I never forgot: "Communication intensity is extraordinary. Two companies known for their no-holds-barred communications in characteristically uncommunicative industries are Exxon and Citibank. We've had the opportunity to observe senior managers in action at both companies. The difference between their behavior and that of their competitors is nothing short of astonishing. They make a presentation, and then the screaming and shouting begin. The questions are unabashed; the flow is free; everyone is involved. Nobody hesitates to cut off the chairman, the president, a board member."*

I just could not foresee the forceful reaction I was about to cause. I gave the group my "read-back" of what I just heard. I said, "If I got this right, the COO will check with the OR nurses tomorrow to determine if they are okay with their supervisor reporting to the CMO. It is unusual to ask employees for permission to have their supervisor report to another executive."

The COO objected vigorously to my characterization of the plan. The criticism lasted for several minutes, and the CEO was frozen.

After the meeting, the CFO tried to teach me about the expected behavior of executive leadership. In effect, he said don't listen to Thomas Peters because his work does not apply to Palomar Health. The CFO said my actions would separate me from the CEO.

"Don't be the catalyst of your own departure," he warned. He knew what he was talking about. But the lesson came too late. My final grade was posted on January 4, 2019—laid off with severance.

Roger Acheatel, a cardiologist with whom I used to make rounds, came to me after he heard of the decision. He told me that my layoff caught a lot of physicians and nurses by surprise. But he pointed out

---

* Thomas J. Peters and Robert H. Waterman Jr., *In Search of Excellence: Lessons from America's Best-Run Companies*, HarperBusiness Essentials (New York: HarperCollins, 2004).

From left to right, Diane Hansen, CEO, and Sheila Brown, COO, Palomar Health, 2018.

that I would make a "soft landing" because I still had my lab position as medical director. Then Roger asked me if I still carried that book with me. He remembered the book!

I immediately pulled it out of my attaché case. The eleventh chapter of Barbara Linney's *A Career Guide for Executive Physicians* is titled "What to Do When Fired." Note that she did not title the chapter "What to Do *If* Fired." I was as prepared for this day as I could be. While the decision was shocking, I learned an important lesson: emotional intelligence is more valuable than Peters's *In Search of Excellence.*

Dr. David Lee

Dr. David Lee is a Harvard graduate and emergency room physician whom I met at the PMC Medical Staff Peer Review Committee. When

I was the CQO, David and I worked closely together. He turned out to be a great mentor and teacher.

My favorite lessons from Dr. Lee occurred when the California Hospital Association distributed its "Data Suite" report cards predicting the quality and safety performance of PMC Escondido and PMC Poway. I was treated to an in-depth analysis of the methodology used to determine our scores. I loved these lessons and couldn't get enough.

I accepted any methodology a rating agency used. My thought was that I needed to learn to live with the agency's system, share the information, and figure out how to improve, but David was more scientific in his approach. He wanted us all to know the limitations of each agency's report card. It was after such a lesson that I realized rating hospitals is a big money-making business in that the companies that issue hospital grades enjoy substantial revenue for their efforts, and few really understand the value of the reports.

Some of the publicly reported quality information provides value to hospitals and patients. Opportunities for improvement can be identified and corrective actions evaluated. Other agencies are like the March of Dimes—trying to reinvent themselves so they don't go out of business with the advent of a polio vaccine. Leapfrog is such a company, and Leapfrog has great marketing skills to promote its cause.

You've heard of the saying "Good enough for government work." I don't believe it. I think our federal government sets the curve for quality reporting. Of course, there is no perfect method, but the Centers for Medicare and Medicaid Services (CMS) has been trying to measure quality and safety since long before many physicians even thought about the concept.

The CMS system is designed to give a single rating to an entire hospital using one to five stars. The system is challenging to comprehend because it uses over fifty metrics with subjective and objective data. To determine the final rating, data are culled from different time intervals depending on the metric being studied and then amalgamated into the final star rating. For example, a hospital's overall star rating for 2018 would be determined based on 2017 data for hospital-acquired infections (and other hospital-acquired conditions) but weighted against operative complications from a performance period dating to 2014. And the methodology changed almost annually.

This is where David came in. I will confess that thirty to sixty minutes with Dr. Lee on an agency's performance report saved me about three days of study. I marveled at how he could reduce a complex subject to one that is easy to grasp. Then I morphed this information into sound bites, and we both taught Palomar Health leadership.

One day, I asked David if his wife, Christine, enjoyed such analytical work. It turns out Christine had graduated from MIT. David looked me right in the eye and said, "At night in bed, she talks data to me."

David is exacting. Each word has meaning, and there is no place for errors of commission or omission. He catches even the smallest of mistakes. His approach to exactness reminds me of a saying I hear from experienced golfers: "One must learn to use the rules of golf to one's advantage."

I once told David that my explanation of the CMS rating system must be shared with all our health system's employees. I asked him to help me by writing a summary. It would be difficult, I told him, because no memo from our office could exceed a single page. The CMS system is indeed complicated, and David did exactly what was asked of him, but it was not what I had envisioned. David brought me a single page with an easy-to-understand explanation of how the CMS system works. But he had used both sides of the single page. My directions had not been explicit. There was room for another interpretation. David used the rules to his benefit and accomplished the requested task. Afterward, I told him that single-page assignments could only utilize a single side of the page.

And consider the example of a Medical Executive Committee meeting that David and I attended. Someone made a motion regarding a contentious issue. The motion was modified "to require two-thirds of the membership for the motion to be carried," and I immediately seconded. David suggested that this was not what we intended. I almost said it was exactly what I intended. David said he believed we meant that for the motion to carry, at least two-thirds of the members must vote for approval. If we stipulated exactly two-thirds of the membership, what would happen when we got 90 percent approval? We would have missed the two-thirds requirement.

One cannot argue with this logic. In this case, we had made an inappropriate assumption. No harm was done. But can you imagine the effect of such an error in computer programming? I remember on the *Tonight Show with Jay Leno*, Jay once talked of a US space launch to one of the planets. The spacecraft never made it because the programmer entered the wrong "units" of measure. It was an error similar to the two-thirds vote requirement. For NASA, this was a multimillion-dollar error. Leno's final comment on the subject was, "This just goes to show you that you don't have to be a rocket scientist to be a rocket scientist." David would have gotten that spacecraft to Mars.

It feels as if David and I have known each other for a lifetime. But we are almost two generations apart. I get reminded of this in humorous ways. I showed David a holiday newspaper story about a lady who had bought her septuagenarian husband a slide rule for Christmas 2018. "Remember how we used these in quantitative analysis lab in college?" I asked. He replied, "My dad had one of those; I used Texas Instruments."

David works in the Emergency Department when he is not the medical quality officer. That's twenty to thirty hours per week in each position. He is the kind of doctor I would have been if I had been blessed with his skills and compassion. To my credit, I recognize my limitations. Compassion in pathology is not usually crucial. Nonetheless, David would never say about me what an internist did years ago: "I've never met a pathologist who wasn't already dead."

Since being laid off from my CQO job, I've missed Dr. Lee's company and wisdom. He is a modest man and would be embarrassed to read my description of him, but I am accurate. I cherish our friendship and all the support he has provided. I won't let that go.

The Grammarians

I don't know what fascinates me about grammar. Most people don't think the rules apply to them if they communicate effectively. Yet I

Dr. David Lee.

am most appreciative when my grammar is corrected. I call this CGI, continuous grammar improvement. When I am uncertain, I turn to Dr. David Lee (see the preceding essay).

David was most helpful on National Boss's Day. I had just received a celebratory card announcing this day of appreciation. I needed to know if Hallmark Cards spelled the day correctly.

David sent me the following email in response to my requested grammar lesson:

My personality constrains me to send you this email because I realize that whatever form of "boss" I wound up jotting in the card we gave you today, it was almost certainly incorrect. I must admit, I don't recall exactly what variant of "boss" I wrote. But when I was handed the card to jot a quick note, I quickly realized that not only had I not known it was Boss's Day today, I didn't know whether it was

> Boss's Day (possessive case, singular noun)
> Bosses Day (subjective case, plural noun) or
> Bosses' Day (possessive case, plural noun)

I had to look it up upon getting home and found out that it is "Boss's Day" (possessive case, singular noun). I'm pretty sure that's not what I wrote.

Anyway, I am thankful for Boss's Day today because I received a grammar lesson out of it!

I needed to share David's lesson with my son, Jeremy, who responded in "Jeremy Style." You'll need an aspirin after you read it:

Odd, Administrative Professionals' day is possessive plural. Come on Hallmark, let's have some consistency!

(Interjection, vocative proper noun, first person plural contraction and subjective noun, imperative infinitive, determinative pronoun, and singular objective noun)

How'd I do?

I responded that my head hurt, but Jeremy went on:

Actually, Wikipedia has both as possessive plural. Hallmark's various websites have Bosses as subjective plural and Admin's as both possessive and subjective plural. Hallmark also has "National Boss Day" cards, which sounds like another holiday all together.

Timeanddate.com has Admin day as subjective plural and
Boss day as possessive singular. This website also shows that
Yom Kippur is a state holiday in . . . TEXAS!?
Where is the authoritative source?

I told you that you would need an aspirin.

Dr. James Bried

James Bried is an orthopedic surgeon whose reputation is such that
patients travel from all over the United States for hip or knee replace-
ments at PMC Poway. His professional and personal accomplishments
could cause "overachievers" like me to feel a touch of envy. Two
points illustrate this best.

As a young boy, and then as an adolescent, I had dreams of playing
baseball in high school and college. Lettering in a sport was a dream
I tried to make happen at Jamaica High School, but I fell short, as I
mention in my essay "On My Obsession with Michigan Football."

Jim Bried was admitted to the University of Arizona as a scholar
and then walked onto the baseball team as a catcher. They asked
him to stay. In addition to a career in which he gave senior citizens a chance at painless mobility, he also coached a baseball
team that went to the Little League World Series in Williamsport,
Pennsylvania.

It's Jim's sense of humor that particularly attracts me. Several
years ago, he gave a presentation to the board of directors at Palomar
Health showcasing the accomplishments of the Orthopedic Center
of Excellence at PMC Poway. He focused on the processes to avoid
postoperative complications, especially hospital-acquired conditions.
He explained to the board that short lengths of stay reduce the chance
of hospital-acquired conditions and save money. Then he showed that
his performance was in the top decile. Just like when E. F. Hutton
talks, everyone listened.

One board member was agitated. She spoke up with an enraged,
indignant air: "How do you explain the mediocre performance of

others in your department?" Dr. Bried paused just for a moment. It was a beautiful pause that accentuated the coming punch line.

Jim turned toward the board member and said her question reminded him of a story. When he was a boy, his dad called the family to the dinner table. Jim was punctual. His father asked him in an accusing manner where his brother was. Jim just shrugged his shoulders as if to say, "I don't know."

It took a moment for the audience to link Dr. Bried's father's question to Genesis 4:9 (NIV):

Then the Lord said to Cain, "Where is your brother Abel?" "I don't know," he replied. "Am I my brother's keeper?"

For me, this was a humorous and tactful reply designed to teach the board member that questions about individual physician performance should be directed to the individual—not to the physician in the top decile.

Jim also provided comic relief when discussing altercations that involve physicians. He said he didn't need an anger management class; he needed people to stop pissing him off. This is especially entertaining because Jim doesn't get pissed off. He is a mentor to his colleagues.

I am thankful for Dr. James Bried. He supported me during difficult times at Palomar Health and was a source of encouragement when I was laid off as CQO in 2019.

Dr. James Bried, 2020.

NINE

Michigan and Dreams of Athleticism

Michigan Men's Football Experience

got excited when I read in an alumni news email that Michigan fantasy football would be returning May 30–31, 2012. Michigan alumni football, or perhaps more officially, the Michigan Men's Football Experience (MMFE), was inaugurated in 2005 when Lloyd Carr was head coach. But it had not been repeated. Rich Rodriguez, who followed Carr as head coach, apparently hadn't been enthusiastic about bringing it back. Who cares about the reason for the hiatus? I had a second chance to be a dreamer. Would I do it?

My first thought was that I traveled too much. I could not afford to be away from the hospital even more. But, as lab manager Tim Barlow said, it was easier to reach me when I was out of town than when I was in the hospital. I decided work was not going to be the excuse that kept me from my fantasy.

What about money? The fantasy costs $5,000. I needed to stop calling it the fantasy. I like that term, but let's face it, we are talking fantasy on a monumental scale. After all, I would be running out on the field at the Big House through the tunnel. Was that worth $5,000?

My first thought was straightforward: when I died, there would be a lot more money in the bank than $5,000. Lack of money could not be a reason for staying home. Furthermore, I could use my United

Mileage Plus Visa card, earn mileage credit toward a free first-class flight somewhere, and deduct a portion of the cost of the football experience as a charitable expense! I was starting to feel philanthropic about joining the team.

I concluded that this was a bargain. I should waste no time. I called Michigan's contact person, Maureen Perdomo. She explained that the event was a fundraiser sponsored by the University of Michigan School of Medicine, Department of Urology, to further promote research on prostate cancer. I told her I would send my application with my $5,000 check.

After three days, I had not heard from Michigan. I started to wonder if my application hadn't been accepted. I called Maureen. She assured me she already had my money, and I was on the team. Wow, I was on the team!

When I attended Jamaica High School in Queens from 1961–64, I tried out for track, baseball, and handball. I got rejected from track because you could not join the team if you ran the one-hundred-yard dash in more than 12.5 seconds. I ran it in 13.0. I asked the coach if I could try to run it again. The coach said I could try as often as I liked. I tried again. It took more than 12.5 seconds, and my track career was over.

Baseball was no different. Handball was tantalizing because they put me on the team in the off-season. But when the season began, all these other guys, some unsavory types, showed up, and they all made the team—not me. More on that later. But Maureen had officially accepted my application to the MMFE. I agree with Arthur Miller that one of the key reasons I love Michigan is that they accepted me.

Sometimes, you may make the team, but life has other plans. One example is my application to the University of Michigan School of Medicine for a residency in pathology in 1972. I explained during my interview with the chairman, Dr. James French, and also his secretary, that should I be fortunate enough to get matched to Michigan in an "early decision," I would not be able to respond in a timely way. I would be in Israel on a four-month fellowship at Tel HaShomar Hospital in Tel Aviv. I said to both of them that if I were offered the position as a resident at Michigan, I would accept. I got accepted.

When I returned home from Israel, I found four letters from Michigan. The first was the acceptance, the second was Michigan's second
request for a reply, the third was the final warning, and the fourth
told me my place was given away. I had returned home too late to
get the position. This may help explain why I felt I had to check with
Maureen to find out if I was accepted for the MMFE. Even fantasies
have rules.

Rules of the experience: Significant others were permitted to
attend registration and have lunch with what was known as Alumni
Team 133. But the players were to have dinner and all subsequent
meals without family and friends. It would be just the team from
that point forward. Parenthetically, at 4:00 p.m. on the first day at
Schembechler Hall, Head Coach Brady Hoke announced that exactly
132 years earlier—at 4:00 p.m., May 30, 1879—Michigan played
its first football game.

I told Dale about the significant-other rule. She agreed she would
bring me to the Sheraton for registration, and then, addressing me
like a schoolboy, she said, "I will drop you off and make sure you
find some friends."

We were told to arrive at the Sheraton Ann Arbor between
10:00 a.m. and noon on Wednesday, May 30. I got there a little
after 10:00 a.m. Things happened fast. I needed Dale to explain to
me some of the details that I was not recalling.

I signed in and was given the agenda for the two days. They
whisked me off to another station where I was given a beautiful leather
duffel bag that had an embossed MMFE logo on the outside and a
thermos inside. I got my jersey with number twenty-four on the back
(the number Willie Mays wore when he played baseball for the New
York Giants). Most important to me was an autographed football
signed by the entire coaching staff, including Hoke. The football had
an inscription: "Game Football presented to Jerry Kolins."

I was told to change into my jersey for my picture. My photograph
was to be projected onto the big screen at the Big House when my
name and number were announced on the public address system before
the game on Thursday. I also paid extra for a video of myself. The
photographer even shot a photo of me posing as a quarterback looking

to pass. The caption of the photo is "Heisman Hopeful, Jerry Kolins." I have since voluntarily relinquished all four years of my eligibility.

Dale reminded me that I must return my jersey after the photo was taken. The jerseys were to be brought to the locker room by the equipment staff to await game day. I wanted to hold on to my jersey, but I got on board with the game plan.

After the photo session, I said hello to Brady Hoke and told him we had almost been neighbors in San Diego before he resigned as head coach at San Diego State to take the Michigan post. (By the way, Hoke returned to the San Diego State Aztecs in 2020.) He lived on Paseo Bonita, a street linking Pacific Beach and La Jolla. We chatted briefly. I was mindful of my teammates who also wanted to say hello to Coach Hoke.

It was not yet noon (at which time, we all were to go into the Michigan Ballroom at the Sheraton for lunch). I already felt I got my money's worth. If they sent me home right then and there, I would have felt this was a superb event. The bell rang. Lunchtime. We all moved into the ballroom.

Lunch was huge and served buffet style. I got in line with Fred Jackson, running back coach. He had coached Anthony Thomas, Chris Perry, and many others. There was roast beef, ham, turkey, and American cheese for sandwiches; coleslaw; potato salad; soda; coffee; and so on. I don't remember all the stuff. I was staring a lot.

Speeches were made after lunch. Coach Hoke addressed us all and introduced his assistant coaches. The buses would leave at 1:15 p.m. exactly. If you were not on the bus at that time, the buses rolled without you. I was always five to ten minutes early for everything.

We were brought to our classroom in Schembechler Hall. The classroom was more luxurious than any I had seen. The seats were upholstered—dark blue, of course, with a yellow block M on the back of every chair. I sat in the back row in an aisle seat. The associate athletic director, Mike Vollmer, addressed us first and said we could not have anyone sitting in the left or right sections of the room. Everyone sits in the center section, and there is to be no space between seats. "This is one team, and we stay together," he said. A few of us were asked to move down to the center. I was obedient.

Next, we got our playbook. The first half had motivational sayings that reminded me of the emotional growth classes at CEDU that Jessica had attended. It did get me pumped up, but I didn't exactly know what I was getting pumped up about. The second half of the playbook was scary. It was filled with plays and formations that made no sense to me. Well, why should it make sense? I don't understand the game.

About a third of the fifty who attended the MMFE had played organized football sometime in their lives. I was in the majority who hadn't. This is one complex sport. My brother, Mark, suggested that Michigan should teach an informal course in football. By that, he meant a noncredit course that teaches students what's happening on Saturday afternoon. A fee could be charged, and I bet the class would be filled. I hardly went to the games when I was a student. Instead, I would go to the library thinking I would get way ahead of everyone else. Later in life, I found out, it doesn't work that way.

We got tours of the weight and conditioning rooms and saw the rehab equipment: hot tubs, cold tubs, and electronic tables that stimulated muscle groups. It just went on and on. This was more complicated than physical chemistry.

On the first afternoon, we went to class. One of the first classes was offense, taught by offensive coordinator Al Borges. He explained the significance of wearing the "pants in the family." Then we broke up into smaller groups according to the position we hoped to play. I chose linebacker, but I didn't really know what that meant. I think now that I should have tried for cornerback. At least I understand what that guy is supposed to do. We listened to the sage Lloyd Carr and the experienced Dave Brandon talk of Michigan.

Carr explained that the player's seat in the classroom is determined by class standing. Seniors sit in the front rows. Front row center can be a highly contested location that had on at least one occasion resulted in an altercation that had required Carr's intervention.

Dave Brandon, athletic director and a past regent of the university, spoke of the importance of the fundraising effort to promote research in prostate cancer. Brandon was treated at Michigan for the disease. His father and grandfather had prostate cancer.

Brady Hoke spoke to us like he would a freshman class. He explained we had three great rivalries at Michigan: Notre Dame is our national rivalry. We also have a great in-state rivalry. The actual name of the school with which we have this great in-state rivalry was not mentioned, although if you were to look in East Lansing, you likely would find it. And then, there is the greatest rivalry in any sport, Michigan and that team from Ohio. At this point, I was so wound up, I would have donated my right kidney to the urology department.

In the evening, there was dinner at the club level of Michigan Stadium. There was a bar that offered cocktails, wine, and beer. The coaches explained that this part of the experience is not similar to the student experience.

During cocktails, I spoke with equipment manager Jon Falk, who has more stories than one can imagine, and each one is captivating. He said Tom Brady once asked him which Big Ten Championship ring he cherished the most. Jon replied, "The next one." Brady, the Michigan quarterback who went on to roll up six Super Bowl wins with the New England Patriots and one Super Bowl victory for the Tampa Bay Buccaneers (2020 NFL season), used the line and gave Jon Falk credit when he was asked which Super Bowl ring meant the most to him.

I also spoke with Gary Moeller, who looked younger than he did when he coached Michigan in the early 1990s. He expressed concerns about the college athletes who make it in the NFL and then are bankrupt five years after their pro careers are over. Moeller's concern for the players showed in his facial expressions.

Dinner at the club level was monumental. I was served a salad followed by clam chowder. Then came the main course: filet mignon, lasagna, and the biggest baked potato I have ever seen. There were platters of vegetables on the table, including asparagus, and I ate about a third of what was served. Dessert was an ice cream sundae. Then the buses took us back to the Sheraton. Hot chocolate and cookies were delivered to every room. I could only take a sip of the hot chocolate. I needed to stop eating and start reading the playbook. I packed the cookies in my duffel bag for consumption after the "big game."

Bed check was at 10:00 p.m. My room did not have bed check because Dale had put the "Do not disturb" sign on the door. Even so, I honored lights out at 11:00 p.m. Dale stayed overnight. I don't think women are permitted to be with the guys before a real game. But Dale decided to sleep with a guy who still had four years of eligibility remaining. It must have been exciting for her.

The next morning, Dale made the "walk of shame" as she left the hotel and headed back to our condo in the Tower Plaza Apartments. John Will, a friend and contractor who had redesigned the condo, explained the walk of shame as coeds returning to their apartments or dorms on Sunday morning after spending Saturday night somewhere else. As objectionable as those words are today, they were used commonly in the fifties and sixties.

The wake-up alarm on game day was a telephone call at 6:00 a.m. Breakfast at 6:30 a.m. Buses roll at 7:15 a.m. For breakfast, we had eggs, sausage, potatoes—the stuff that made Lipitor a blockbuster. I walked by a small table that had cereal. I peeked and walked away. What if someone saw me?

The buses brought us to our locker rooms. Imagine what I was feeling when I saw my name on the locker and my jersey hanging in plain view. Now I was ready to donate my other kidney.

We practiced outdoors next to the indoor practice field that had opened about two years earlier. I played receiver as a Z, X, or ZB. Coach Jeff Hecklinski was very patient with me. A few times as ZB, I lined up five yards behind the line of scrimmage instead of just off the line. On the last play of practice, I ran a mediocre route, cut into the middle, and was tripped by a defensive player. I still don't know where the guy came from. I thought I was out there alone—I was so focused on the ball. By the way, the ball was not thrown to me. I fell, got banged up, and was not even in the play.

Probably the most patient and direct teacher was Mark Smith, who coached linebackers. When trying to explain some unnatural, complicated moves that we had to perform quickly, he asked if we all got it. One guy yelled in no uncertain terms, "Yes, we do!" But Coach Smitty said, "No, you don't." There is no way we could have mastered that so quickly.

After practice, we boarded the buses for the locker room. We took showers and dressed for lunch at the Campus Inn Huron Ballroom. Two plates were placed, one on top of the other, at every seat. The top plate was filled with chicken, eggs, and hash brown potatoes. In the center of the table were huge platters of spaghetti. You were supposed to let the waitstaff take your first plate, revealing the clean plate underneath, which was to be used for spaghetti. I never got that far.

I sat next to a guy who had graduated in 2010. I graduated in 1968. Brady Hoke sat at my table for a while. He explained to us all that lunch before a game is solemn. There is not much talking. We were loud. We were too excited about surviving morning practice.

After lunch, we moved into the Regency Ballroom of the Campus Inn for film review. In our case, as with the real team, film is always reviewed twice—once from a defensive perspective and then from an offensive viewpoint. Our morning practice session was videotaped. The first review was by Greg Mattison, defensive coordinator, who explained the opportunities for improvement on defense. Then Al Borges, offensive coordinator, analyzed the same film with a complete focus on offense. He stopped the video and circled my fall. "Will someone tell this guy to fall like an athlete?" he asked. I loved being singled out, even if it was because I'm clumsy. When I got back to San Diego, I had X-rays of my chest. I still don't believe the radiologist who said my ribs were not fractured. When the radiologist saw the look of disappointment on my face, he tried to console me by saying it is possible to miss a hairline fracture. But my friend Art Silvergleid says you cannot have a hairline fracture if you do not have a hairline.

During the offensive film review and analysis, I was sitting next to Adam Stanovich, an offensive lineman at Michigan who had played in the NFL. He asked me if I saw that guy fall. Somewhat embarrassingly, I told him that guy was me. After film review, we left the Campus Inn to board the buses. This turned out to be the most emotionally intense experience of the two days—even more than running through the tunnel and touching the banner at midfield.

When I joined the team to walk through the doors of the hotel to the outside, the Campus Inn staff was lined up on the right and left, cheering us onward. I hope no one saw the tears in my eyes. For a moment, I thought I was an athlete. It was beautiful. I was being encouraged by total strangers who were clapping their hands and shouting "Go Blue!" as I got on the bus. I was sorry I hadn't come with a third kidney.

Because I was tripped in practice, I was hurting, but I kept it to myself. I had to run out through the tunnel onto the field, jump up to touch the banner, and join the team on the sidelines. I did it. From the sidelines, I heard "Number twenty-four, from La Jolla, California, Jerry Kolins!" I ran from the sidelines to center field, and I think I heard my wife cheer.

I had worried for weeks about whether I would be able to leap high enough to reach the "Go Blue—M Club Supports You" banner. When I ran out on the field, I noticed the banner was on shorter poles. Michigan understood its customer. I could reach this pennant,

I'm living a dream at the Big House.

Snagging a pass at practice. If only
I could learn to keep my eye on the
ball, there would be more completed
passes. Go Blue!

but I paced myself to be sure I did not jump too early. I did a two-hand touch.

Then the game began. We had referees dressed in their zebra uniforms. Coaches Hoke, Moeller, and Carr watched us all. I was so happy when it was announced that the game was over. I was exhausted. Now it was time for our team photo.

John Will showed up and tried to get Lloyd Carr to autograph one of the cones we used on the field to help guide our practice. John was recognized as an "outside agitator." You know what I mean. The term was first used in Mike Nichols's 1967 movie *The Graduate*. Actor Norman Fell asks Dustin Hoffman if he is one, with Richard Dreyfuss overlooking the interrogation.

After the game and photos, I went home and dreamed of making one-handed catches in the back of the end zone. I wear my jersey to bed now.

Postscript: You may ask why all this means so much to me. Broadcaster Bob Ufer explained it best: "Football is the religion, and Saturday is the holy day of obligation."

On My Obsession with Michigan Football

I often ask myself why I care about the Michigan football program. I never played the game. As I've said, in high school, I wanted to letter in a sport—any sport. I tried out for baseball. I didn't make it. I made the varsity handball team in the off-season. Boy, was I excited! What I didn't know was that the really good players never show up for the off-season, because there were no competitive games then. I practiced and showed up, figuring it would improve my chances of lettering in the spring. But there was no place for me when the season started. I was not good enough. These guys who only showed up in the spring were the best I ever saw. I never played again.

When I was an undergraduate student at Michigan, I attended two Michigan football games. I remember Michigan playing Michigan State University (MSU) in 1967. My roommate said I had to go to this game if I ever wanted to say I had graduated from Michigan. Michigan had all but lost before halftime. And that's when I left the stadium. In my junior year, I watched Michigan lose to Purdue 22–21. Bob Griese, who quarterbacked Purdue, later quarterbacked the Miami Dolphins to two consecutive Super Bowl championships. Brian Griese, who quarterbacked Michigan to a national championship in 1997, is Bob Griese's son. At the 1966 Purdue game, Michigan had the ball in Purdue territory with only a few seconds remaining. A thirty-five-yard field goal would win it, but the ball did not reach the end zone. I graduated and went to medical school—just like I had always wanted.

After I left Michigan, I got consumed by the game. Since I attended medical school at Wayne State University in Detroit, it was easy to return to Ann Arbor. During my freshman year of medical school, in 1968, Michigan played Ohio State in Columbus. I listened on the radio because not much college football was televised then, and of course, there was no cable TV or Big Ten Network. Ohio State was no. 1 in the country in 1968, but at halftime, the score was close, 21–14 in Ohio State's favor. The Buckeyes dominated the second half and, with less than a minute remaining in the game, scored a touchdown that pushed their lead to 48–14. Then, even though up by thirty-four points, Ohio went for a two-point conversion and made it! The final score was 50–14. For a very short time, I wondered why Woody Hayes went for two with only seconds left. I didn't wonder for long because, as legend has it, that was the first question the press asked him after the game. Woody said he went for two because the referees wouldn't let him go for three. This was entertaining. There was something going on between Michigan and Ohio State that intrigued me.

During my sophomore year in medical school, in 1969, I went to two Michigan football games. I watched Michigan lose to MSU in East Lansing. I still remember an MSU kickoff to one of Michigan's most accomplished running backs. He caught the ball on the one-foot line, took a step back into the end zone, and placed his knee on the ground. That is called a safety. MSU got two points and the ball back. We lost a game that we should have won. That made the MSU rivalry even more exciting. And it was not the last time Michigan lost to an inferior team. Even MSU fans do not believe they won the 2015 contest.

We need a brief sidebar. In 2018, John Bacon, the author of several *New York Times* best sellers, explained the difference between Michigan versus Notre Dame football, Michigan versus Ohio State football, and Michigan versus Michigan State football: In a Michigan–Notre Dame game, the players and the fans respect each other. In a Michigan–Ohio State game, the players respect each other, and the fans hate each other. In a Michigan–Michigan State game, the players and the fans hate each other. That summary captures the cultures of these rivalries. Yet Michigan will be first to admit that MSU is the little brother compared to the unrivaled competition between Michigan and Ohio State. This competition has always been intense, but it reached new levels thanks to Woody Hayes and Bo Schembechler. Why the hell would I care?

My answer may not be completely satisfying, but it is an attempt to understand myself. Let me explain with help from Edward O. Wilson.

He is a Harvard biologist who has written Pulitzer Prize–winning books that attempt to answer these difficult questions: Is there a judgmental God? What is the meaning of human existence? Wilson answers the first question in his book *Consilience*. This is no easy read. He writes a chapter in which he explains why there absolutely must be a judgmental God. It is a convincing chapter. The subsequent chapter outlines the argument against the existence of a judgmental God. That argument is irrefutable. Yet Wilson welcomes the reader to challenge his position. In his book *The Meaning of Human Existence*, Wilson makes his position clear that humans need a society in order to survive, which is unusual among mammals. Religion is not a prerequisite for society, though most of us don't accept this.

What does this have to do with Michigan football? Humans need a structured society; we need to belong to a group. If you believe in a judgmental God, you have a religion to bring you together. If you cherish your immediate family, they may provide the sense of belonging your genetic material demands. Your professional career may also provide this required sense of belonging. What happens to those who believe the universe can be explained without conjuring up a God? What happens to those who feel neither family nor profession fills the void that DNA mandates? Michigan football is my religion.

As a religion, Michigan football provides many levels of satisfaction. When I go to Michigan Stadium, I sit with over one hundred thousand folks who I don't know. And I like that. Actually, I prefer that. But we all have something in common: we feel connected to the University of Michigan through the football team. The team brings us together on Saturday the same way religion brings the masses to church on Sunday. And we are not really one hundred thousand people watching a game; we are about twenty-five thousand groups of three to five folks who look forward to seeing each other six or seven times a year for life's renewal. We will even gift to these otherwise strangers our personal and precious team souvenirs as we near the end of our lives.

Roy sat next to me in Section 41 for years. He was a World War II veteran. He knew my love for Michigan and its football team. One day, he gave me a signed photo of Tom Harmon, Michigan's first Heisman Trophy winner, and his ticket to the 1930 Michigan-Illinois football game. I have them both framed and hanging in my Ann Arbor condo. That ticket cost three dollars in 1930. Today it would be more than twenty times that. But why would Roy give this to me? He knew I would protect his cherished, precious mementos. They needed protection, and I could provide it. Perhaps the religious among us would call these relics.

Can our DNA control us the way I described previously? I don't know. But I became a believer in 1969. The year after Woody Hayes went for two because they would not let him go for three, Michigan played Ohio State at home. It was November 22, 1969. I was there in the end zone seats. OSU was no. 1 in the country and had been since September 1968. Another OSU victory was predicted, but Michigan was not to be denied. At halftime, the score was Michigan 24, Ohio State 12. During the second half of the game, neither team scored a point. The Mets were not the only miracle in 1969. And I found a place to belong.

Postscript: I have lived in La Jolla, California, and been a Michigan football season ticket holder since 1977. Between 1977 and 1997 (the year Michigan won the national championship), I attended up to three games a year. Since 2016, I have leased a suite over the freshman section. I haven't missed a home game since. And United Airlines really appreciates that!

From *The Meaning of Human Existence* by Edward O. Wilson:

All things being equal (fortunately things are seldom equal, not exactly), people prefer to be with others who look like them, speak the same dialect, and hold the same beliefs. An amplification of this evidently inborn predisposition leads with frightening ease to racism and religious bigotry. Then, also with frightening ease, good people do bad things. I know this truth from experience, having grown up in the Deep South during the 1930s and 1940s.

It might be supposed that the human condition is so distinctive and came so late in the history of life on Earth as to suggest the hand of a divine creator. Yet, as I've stressed, in a critical sense the human achievement was not unique at all. Biologists have identified at the time of this writing twenty evolutionary lines in the modern-world fauna that attained advanced social life based on some degree of altruistic division of labor. Most arose in the insects. Several were independent origins in marine shrimp, and three appeared among the mammals—that is, in two African mole rats, and us. All reached this level through the same narrow gateway: solitary individuals, or mated pairs, or small groups of individuals built nests and foraged from the nest for food with which they progressively raised their offspring to maturity.

Probably at this point, during the habiline period, a conflict ensued between individual-level selection, with individuals competing with other individuals in the same group, on the one side, and group-level selection, with competition among groups, on the other. The latter force promoted altruism and cooperation among all the group members. It led to innate group-wide morality and a sense of conscience and honor. The competition between the two forces can be succinctly expressed as follows: Within groups selfish individuals beat altruistic individuals, but groups of altruists beat groups of selfish individuals. Or, risking oversimplification, individual selection promoted sin, while group selection promoted virtue.

> —Edward O. Wilson, *The Meaning of Human Existence*
> (New York: Liveright, 2014)

Michigan Meshuggaas

My parents thought of my University of Michigan obsession as Michigan meshuggaas. The word is Yiddish for "madness." A person who is described as mad is a meshuggener. It has been said that if you don't have anything nice to say, then say it in Yiddish.

But even in English, I consider what happened in spring 2019 to be an insult. Unintentional, yes, and noticeable only to those whose Michigan madness is as severe as mine, but still an insult. To understand it, you must know about fraud, bribery, and elite universities.

QS World University Rankings is an organization that ranks the world's universities. The score is based on six metrics: academic reputation (40 percent), employer reputation (10 percent), faculty-student ratio (20 percent), citations per faculty (20 percent), international faculty ratio (5 percent), and international student ratio (5 percent). Organizations that rank universities, and there are many, have different motives. And the value of these rankings is highly questionable. Nonetheless, the rankings are entertaining. So here are a few words on the methodology used by QS.

Academic reputation is measured using a survey tool. The survey is completed by "over 94,000 individuals in the higher education space regarding teaching and research quality at the world's universities. In doing so, it has been the world's largest survey of academic opinion, and, in terms of size and scope, is an unparalleled means of measuring sentiment in the academic community." Employer reputation is a survey measurement of "45,000 employers asked to identify those institutions from which they source the most competent, innovative, effective graduates."* The QS website states that the QS Employer Survey is the world's largest of its kind. Obviously, academic and employer reputation are subjective metrics. The remaining four metrics are objective, though their value will vary depending on the reader.

Michigan was rated in 2020 as the best public university in the United States and no. 21 in the world (including both public and private schools). The second-highest-rated public university in the United States was the University of California, Berkeley, which came in at no. 28 in the world. Perhaps not surprising is the fact that the United States and the United Kingdom secured nine of the top ten slots in the

---

* "QS World University Rankings," QS TopUniversities, accessed April 28, 2021, https://www.topuniversities.com/university-rankings/world-university-rankings/2020.

After another victory over Ohio State, this time 40–34, on November 26, 2011.

world rankings, with MIT no. 1, Stanford no. 2, and Harvard no. 3. Next in order were the University of Oxford, California Institute of Technology, and the Swiss Federal Institute of Technology (the only country other than the United States and the United Kingdom to have a university in the top ten).

Rounding out the top ten were Cambridge, University College London, Imperial College London, and the University of Chicago, "where fun goes to die."*

---

* This is a line Anna Kendrick says to Ben Affleck in the movie *The Accountant*. It is worth seeing. You may also be wondering where Michigan's Big Ten rivals stand in the QS World University Rankings. When looking at the overall rankings that include private and public universities, Ohio State is ranked no. 101 (higher than I thought), Michigan State no. 144 (just about right), Northwestern no. 31 (no surprise), and competitive Wisconsin ranked no. 56.

Michigan meshuggaas often manifests itself in the wearing of maize-and-blue clothing.

The survey helps justify my obsession with Michigan—no. 1 public university in the United States, and proud of it! So why do I feel insulted?

Federal prosecutors in Boston unsealed a criminal complaint on March 12, 2019, that charged fifty people with conspiracy to commit mail fraud and honest services mail fraud. The CliffsNotes summary of the indictment is that dozens of parents tried to bribe colleges, universities, and coaches to get their kids into the elite school of their choice. This was shocking to me. Not the bribery charges, but that prosecutors referred to schools like Wake Forest, the University of Texas, and the University of Southern California as elite schools. Who are they kidding?

OK, I'm a snob about Michigan. Some actress and her fashion designer husband paid $500,000 to a fixer to get their twins into USC on a rowing scholarship, though the kids never participated in the sport. But my snobbery only goes so far. I would go to USC for a college education—but only if they gave me $500,000.

Autumn in Ann Arbor, looking east from our Tower Plaza condominium.

Don't get me wrong. Some of the schools involved in the scandal have earned the right to be described as elite. Stanford, UCLA, and Yale are all elite in my book. But I checked QS World Rankings on Wake Forest, Texas, and USC. They ranked 398, 65, and 129, respectively. Then came the biggest insult. After the story broke, I boasted with immature pride that you wouldn't find Michigan on a list of schools that had committed a felony. A colleague said that was because the parents only targeted elite universities in the United States. That's the guy who insulted me.

Sweet Stories

The University of Michigan athletic department has me figured out. They called in late 2015 to tell me they had heard I may be interested in a suite for the 2016 football season. How sweet it is! They called because I had filled out some online form expressing interest, but I hadn't believed I would ever hear from them. Now I had my chance to engage in extreme fiscal irresponsibility.

To lease a suite costs about $72,000 per year if you don't want the parking pass. With only seven home games a season, that is over $10,000 per game. But at the time this opportunity presented itself, I was sixty-eight. My life was not at the two-minute warning, but I was in the fourth quarter. Why did I work so hard all my life? What was the money for? It was time to spend it, I reasoned.

Then I remembered my friend Michael Orlando. We were coresidents at the National Institutes of Health (NIH) in pathology. He had retired to Davidson, North Carolina. Recently, I talked him into flying to Chicago to dine at Alinea. Dinner was about $750 per person. That caused Michael to pause. I said we were getting older every day, so it was time to spend the money. Michael said he remembered me saying that same thing in 1975 at the NIH when I didn't have money. He went on to admit that anytime I came up with an idea, he knew we are going to have a memorable adventure—and that he would need to take out another mortgage.

Well, I didn't need another mortgage to lease the suite. I had two jobs in 2015, vice president of patient experience and medical director of laboratories at Palomar Health. I could lease the suite and, like McDonald's once said, go home with change. I did it.

I read the terms of the agreement after I signed the papers. Yes, I was that excited. Turns out, there were sixteen tickets for each suite that came with the deal. Catering costs extra, of course. But sixteen tickets! I didn't know sixteen people. I envisioned myself in the suite with just my brother looking down on the field the way Statler and Waldorf of the Muppets looked down from the balcony onto the orchestra.

Here are a few sweet stories from the first year in the suite.

SUITE STORY NO. 1

I wanted to arrive early for the Illinois game on October 22, 2016. Dale and the rest of my family said they would meet me at the game. I enjoyed walking around the stadium, hunting for my brick,* and watching the festivities unfold. As I walked from Hoover Avenue toward the stadium, I saw a small girl with her daddy. She was on a skateboard. She was young enough so that both feet easily fit side by side. Her dad was pulling her toward the stadium. I stopped to take a picture of the stadium and the people milling about, as I usually do. I could not help but overhear their conversation.

DADDY: Do you see that building straight ahead? That is Michigan Stadium. That is where they play those games we watch on TV at home. It is all happening right in there.

LITTLE GIRL: Let's go in there. We should see them play.

DADDY: You cannot just go in. You need tickets to get in.

LITTLE GIRL: Well, let's get tickets!

DADDY: Tickets cost money.

LITTLE GIRL: Daddy, let's get money!

DADDY: You must save your money and then buy the tickets. We cannot do that now.

I walked toward the stadium, seeing that Daddy's plan was to show her the turnstiles and then leave. I stopped. Turned to walk over to him. At first, I thought it would be strange to approach them and offer them tickets. But I had sixteen! "Excuse me," I said. "We don't know each other, and we may have nothing in common other than our love for Michigan. I have tickets to the Maryland game I can give you. If you are comfortable giving me your US mailing address, I will mail the tickets to you."

I met Dennis and his wife, Ashley, and their daughter, Emory, age four, on November 5, 2016, at the Maryland game. We won 59–3.

---

* I bought a commemorative brick honoring Bo Schembechler and the 1969 team as part of a fundraiser, and it is located inside the stadium gates at the southwest corner.

SUITE STORY NO. 2

I have grown fond of the Bill and Cecilia Fileti family. Like John Bacon says, Michigan Stadium is not filled with 114,000 fans. It is filled with 20,000 unique families that see each other in many cases only six or seven times a year and then at weddings, anniversaries, and funerals. I had met Bill Fileti a few years before I had the suite, when I changed seats to Section 417. There was something about him I found endearing. He watched the game with the same emotions on his face that I showed. I told him recently that he reminded me of myself, only handsome. I meant that. And he had a gentle voice that New Yorkers are not used to experiencing.

When I told him I had decided to get a suite that overlooked the student section, his first question to me was, "Does this mean we won't be seeing each other?" I immediately gave him a set of fourth-quarter passes so he could join me in the fourth quarter of every game. In 2016, Bill had a health setback and could not walk well enough to negotiate the stairs to Section 417. But the suite is adjacent to an elevator. How perfect was that? For the Wisconsin game on October 1, 2016, I suggested that the Fileti family reunion begin in the suite before the 3:30 p.m. game. I delivered ten tickets. I reminded him that the suite held sixteen people and that I didn't know sixteen people. Thank goodness I knew people who did know sixteen people.

The Fileti family reunion was great, and I declared myself an honorary family member. Bill died of glioblastoma multiforme in 2017. I went to the funeral and had a chance to speak about my relationship with him. I honored Bill by sponsoring the Michigan Marching Band halftime show at the Michigan–Ohio State game of 2019. The Fileti family would get a photo of the band formation honoring Bill.

SUITE STORY NO. 3

When Dale and I go to Ann Arbor for a football game, dinner on Friday before the game is usually just the two of us. Group activities are reserved for Saturday, and we return to San Diego Sunday morning. But Cecilia Fileti told us about Mikette Bistro and Bar, a new restaurant in Ann Arbor known for great seafood and very reasonable prices (that means "attractive to students"). She said it was noisy, but we might still love it. We gave it a try on October 21, 2016.

We sat in a section where the tables were so close that a person could not pass between them. The couple to my right ordered a dish that fascinated Dale. She asked them what they had ordered, a surprising question to me because we were protective of our space and respected the space of others. A discussion ensued. Caleb Collier, who was seated at the next table, began to tell me about his family.

His wife, Laura, had a great-grandfather who was a farmer in Michigan in the 1920s. The coach of the Michigan football team at that time, Fielding Yost, who was recruited from Princeton, asked farmers to help dig the hole for Michigan Stadium.* Laura's great-grandfather helped dig the hole.

Then Laura and Caleb spoke of her grandfather. He hadn't missed attending a home game until his health interfered. He hadn't been to a game in years, though Caleb assured me that he hadn't missed one on TV. I gave them four tickets so that Caleb, Laura, Grandma, and Grandpa could attend. I explained the elevator situation, just as I shared with the Fileti family, and the wheelchair accommodations. Grandpa would not leave the suite until he told me the story of his dad digging the hole.

Suite stories are possible only because I am fiscally irresponsible. Who would have guessed that's a good thing!

Ann Arbor and John Will

Our entire family went to Michigan for a three-day weekend in 1990. My mom and dad were staying with my brother, Mark, and my sister-in-law, Maria, in Grosse Pointe. In those days, Dale and I stayed at the Ritz-Carlton in Dearborn. Jeremy and I went to the game

---

* Though Michigan Stadium can accommodate over 115,000 and did so for the 2013 Notre Dame game, with 115,109 attendees, the stadium has a low profile because it is mostly underground.

on Saturday. The plan was to enjoy the game and immediately get back to the hotel, where we would meet my parents, Mark, Maria, Dale, and Jessica. Dinner was to be in the Ritz-Carlton dining room.

After the game, I changed the plan. I told Jeremy I wanted to visit a place that had captivated me in the 1960s. "Let's see what Tower Plaza looks like today," I suggested. We walked the mile from Michigan Stadium to Tower Plaza, and I bought Unit 17C at 555 East William Street in Ann Arbor for $98,500. I was excited and a little nervous. This certainly was an impetuous decision, but it was also a dream come true. Jeremy and I would be late for dinner, but I was so excited that I really didn't care about dinner and figured the family would begin without us.

When we arrived at the restaurant, I was eager to share the happenings of the day, but we were met with hostility. I should say that I was met with hostility; Jeremy was an innocent bystander. My brother was furious about my late arrival. I remember being perplexed. I never expected anyone to be inconvenienced by my late arrival, and I was going to own a place in Ann Arbor. Nonetheless, I suspect some fraternal bitterness remains to this day.

All this was necessary for fate to introduce me to John Will. John had the reputation of doing magic with remodeling projects, and I hired him to transform the Tower Plaza condo. He finished 17C in July 1996, just in time for football season. My mom and dad, John, Christina, Dale, and I met in the unit that summer. I was about to see the space for the first time after spending thousands of dollars to remodel it. I recall using a cardboard box as a table for our drinks, since not all the furniture had arrived yet. This was a new chapter in my life, and John was about to make it special.

It is hard to fully understand what fascinated me most about John. Maybe it's like being served pablum every evening for dinner and someone shows up with the first pizza you ever tasted. John and I often looked at the same event but came away with different conclusions.

John enjoys playing tricks on my brain. He would ask, "Are there any hypothetical questions?" It took me a long time to get the joke. Then there was the time John said he couldn't finish the remodel unless we turned Tower Plaza counterclockwise. Even today that explanation of this remodeling challenge hurts my head. Apparently, in trying to bolt down something in the bathroom, it was physically impossible to turn the screw. So John offered the only other option: let's rotate the building around the bolt.

One of my favorite discussions with John occurred at the Gandy Dancer, a restaurant in Ann Arbor. In February 2006, Vice President Dick Cheney accidentally shot a fellow member of his quail hunting party, attorney Harry Whittington, on a ranch in Texas. I told John that it didn't get much more embarrassing than that. John disagreed and said the guy was lucky Cheney shot him.

Are you kidding me? How does one say blasting a friend on a hunting trip is a lucky experience for the victim? Then came John's explanation: The victim of Dick Cheney's shotgun was immediately brought to the hospital for medical attention. While in the hospital, the patient had a heart attack. John said that if Cheney didn't shoot the guy, he probably would have died of a heart attack on the hunting trip. But the gunshot wound put the guy in the only place that could save his life, the hospital.

Another day, I called John and asked if he could fix one of our closet doors. He asked me what was wrong. I said when I opened the door it didn't stay open, and it closed by itself in just a few seconds. John declared this the perfect door. "There is no need to make the effort to close the door," he said. "The door will take care of that chore for you. Therefore, there is nothing to fix!"

At an Italian restaurant one evening, the waiter brought us pasta puttanesca. The waiter said it was "the best puttanesca you're going to get." I was flattered. I figured I was about to enjoy the best pasta in the world. John said I had misunderstood the waiter: "The really good puttanesca is going to someone else, and this pasta is as good as they care to give you."

We upgraded our condo from 17C to 23JK in October 2004, the best Ann Arbor decision we ever made. But again, the plan needed John Will. In all fairness, John and Dale were the perfect duo on this project, with as Dale the interior designer. The two of them worked together to design a great room with a spectacular view of the Big House. This decision required the loss of one of the two bathrooms.

John Will.

And walls were removed and rebuilt in different locations. My dad thought it a bad business decision. But John's superb work made it an easy decision. Besides, this entire project was not to be a "flip." This was a place for a lifetime.

I go to Ann Arbor seven to nine times a year and enjoy the view of the campus that was the cause of much anxiety from 1965 to 1968. But after graduation, I always dreamed of returning for play instead of study. My dream was to go to Michigan Stadium, and the next day, I would not go to the library. Now I visit libraries on other Big Ten campuses. All this is fun because, at the end of the semester, there is no final examination for me.

More recently, I decided to install a Wi-Fi printer in 23JK. I did it in about ninety minutes including cleanup. All the printer functions work as designed. Dale insisted that I place the printer on the desk located in our bedroom. But there was a movable shelf screwed in place and the screws needed to be removed so the printer would fit where it belonged. I was only able to remove one of the four screws.

I texted John and told him what had happened. He texted back, "You successfully removed a screw. Now get some rest, Jerry."

There is one lesson John taught me that I will never forget. One day, I was feeling sorry for myself. John said, "Don't. I too was thinking about feeling sorry for myself, but that's a slippery slope."

John is all about attitude, and his attitude is rejuvenating—like pizza.

Postscript: John Will's reputation for his craft extends throughout the Ann Arbor vicinity. The prolific writer John Bacon spoke in La Jolla to local alumni about his book *Endzone: The Rise, Fall, and Return of Michigan Football.* I said hello and mentioned that we had a mutual friend in Ann Arbor, John Will. Bacon replied that John's work was second to none. He was seeking John's talent for a home remodel.

TEN

Daydreaming

Mamma Mia

I am shamelessly captivated by the musical *Mamma Mia*. The movie is written around the songs of Abba. I loved it, but when tears came to my eyes in certain scenes, I stopped watching, looked into my pants, and was thankful I was still a man!

So I got to thinking, *Why don't I write a musical?* It would be a story about a high school boy who expresses his love to his girl, assuming she will embrace and reciprocate the feelings. It would perhaps open with Frankie Valli's song "Sherry." An alternative could be the Five Satins singing "In the Still of the Night."

The season is spring. But summer is around the corner, and they will be separated. He suggests they make a pledge. Brian Hyland's song "Sealed with a Kiss" is perfect. She does feel strongly about this guy, so she sings "Please Mr. Postman" by the Marvelettes. The US Postal Service, not sensitive to the emotions of the two high school kids, doesn't deliver the letter. The boy is forced to sing "Return to Sender" by Elvis Presley.

It is clear things are not going well. We have trouble. Yes, there is "Trouble in Paradise," sung by the Crests.*

---

* Johnny Maestro, the Italian American leader of the group, brought together African Americans, Hispanics, and Caucasians. Amazing for the mid-1950s.

The boy is inconsolable. Pavarotti expresses the boy's emotions with "La donna è mobile." The Righteous Brothers sing "You've Lost That Lovin' Feeling," and the boy is shattered to learn his love is fickle. Dion and the Belmonts sing "Runaround Sue."

He has second thoughts. Maybe there is another explanation for all the events. He considers the words of Billy Joel: "That's Not Her Style." He pleads for her to be gentle through Elvis's song "Don't Be Cruel." He dreams of that "One Summer Night" by the Danleers.

Still, he doesn't understand his emotions and proclaims "I Wonder Why (I Love You like I Do)" by Dion and the Belmonts. We then go to Mozart's *The Marriage of Figaro* for "Voi che sapete." This aria was part of the score in *The Shawshank Redemption*. I am not sure what it means. We have a girl playing the role of a young man singing to a woman! The music speaks to the heart. The boy (played by a girl) is consumed by love for a countess. Remember, this opera was written in the eighteenth century.

They meet years later at a dance. He suggests that she "Save the Last Dance for Me" by the Drifters. Dean Martin sings "Sway," and we hear the violins long before it begins. The Duprees make it clear what is going on with "You Belong to Me." Leonard Cohen sings "Dance Me to the End of Love." The story ends with Dean Martin singing "That's Amore."

But, to keep it camp, in the background, if you listen carefully as you walk out of the theater, you can hear Sam the Sham and the Pharaohs singing "Li'l Red Riding Hood."

Airline Etiquette

Let's turn to *Merriam-Webster*'s for the definition of *etiquette*: "the conduct or procedure required by good breeding or prescribed by authority to be observed in social or official life." Now let's compare my highly biased view of the 1960s with the twenty-first century.

The '60s was a time of teaching social responsibility. The entire country needed the lesson, and the Civil Rights Act of 1964 pre-scribed the behavior. The youth of the time brought us the musical

Hair. We were struggling to understand cruel behavior. "How can people be so heartless? How can people be so cruel? Easy to be hard. Easy to be cold . . ."

I sometimes think the golden rule needs modification. The rule states, "Treat others as you would wish to be treated." It's a good rule. But perhaps it's time to incorporate a component of treating others as they would like to be treated. Simple courtesy works for me.

Dale told me of an event that occurred in Warwick's bookstore in La Jolla. An elderly woman was attempting to choose a birthday card or some such greeting card when a young girl's cell phone rang. The girl began a conversation in a loud and disturbing voice. The elderly woman had the courage to ask the young girl to please take the phone call outside. The noise was disturbing. Without skipping a beat, the spoiled brat retorted, "Get used to it. Times have changed. This is the new world." And she continued with her conversation in her rude and entitled manner.

On a United Airlines flight about a year ago, an elderly woman sat next to me. The man in front of her moved his seat backward. The seatback appeared to rest almost on the lady's lap. She said nothing until her dinner arrived. The lady could not lower her tray table because of the extreme angle of the seatback in front of her. She tapped the gentleman's shoulder and asked him to please pull up his seatback. He did it.

But how do we handle someone who refuses to cooperate, such as the ill-mannered girl in Warwick's? Here is my solution for airlines: Passengers are told in advance about a fee linked to reclining one's seat. In front of each seat is a device that permits you to swipe your credit card. The amount you choose to pay determines how far back your seat will recline (within safety limitations, of course).

Here is the exciting part. After you swipe your card, a touch screen has a pop-up that asks if you wish to control your seat or the seat in front of you. If you choose the seat in front, your credit card will be charged a specified amount. At that point, the seat in front of you moves into the upright position. And 90 percent of the amount your credit card was assessed is immediately credited to the passenger who is in front of you.

The person who is sitting in front of you does not have to accept this proactive and intrusive behavior. Remember, we are in the twenty-first century. It's all about "me." So to rectify any perceived wrong, the touch screen in front of the passenger whose seatback you control lights up with a question: Would you like to recline your seat to the previous position? The passenger would also be reminded that his credit card just received dollars from the person who is sitting behind him. If the passenger still wants to recline, the cost of reclining the seat is twice what the other passenger paid to get the seat upright. Should the passenger decide to pay and recline, the passenger who once again has the seatback in his or her lap has a choice: keep the money or pay double to have the seat upright.

The exciting part of this plan is that the cycle does not end until a passenger decides not to pay any more money or is happy with the dollars earned in the game. Eventually, a passenger may reason, "I earned enough money on this transaction; I will leave the seat alone." Everyone wins, including the airline, which keeps 10 percent of each transaction.

The process also helps determine the value of a little space in cramped quarters. Airlines can use this information to set pricing and establish optimal interior design.

I have solutions to a lot of the world's problems. Just ask me.

ELEVEN

Friends

Ian Lazarus and My First
College Baseball Game

I met Ian Lazarus when I was medical director and COO of the American Red Cross Blood Services Division in San Diego. That was around 2003. He gave a talk on Six Sigma. I was not familiar with this quality tool at the time, but I remember Ian started his lecture by saying that many people ask about it: "Who is Sigma, and why is she sick?" they ask. Those sentences captivated my attention.

If you read the biography of Jack Welch, former CEO of General Electric (1981–2001), he credits Six Sigma with the success of his administration. If you are talking about a quality process, Six Sigma demands no more than about 3.4 mistakes in 1 million attempts to get it right. That's impressive performance. In health care, performance at the third sigma is common, and the fourth sigma is rare. There is a lot of work to do. Ian was a mentor to me, though he may not think of himself that way.

After working with Ian for a few months, I was delighted to learn that he graduated from the University of Michigan with a master's in public health. He makes a compelling argument for excellence. I needed to connect.

Ian and I worked together on improving a process at Palomar Health that benefits patients with chest pain. Ian published this work, and I was proud to have worked with him. We have been communicating for over fifteen years. On Saturday, June 8, 2019, I got a text from him that read, "Incredible game. I'll be home after 12:30 tmrw. Hope you can drive up and we can take the Tesla to LA."

Ian was referring to the super regionals in college baseball. Michigan had not been to the College World Series in Omaha since 1984, and he was hoping we would beat the no. 1 team in the country, UCLA, for the right to go again.

Whoever wins two out of three games goes to the series. I was conflicted. Michigan won the first game, but UCLA was the top team in the country. You don't give them a chance to come back after a loss. They are too good.

I watched the second game on TV. UCLA beat Michigan by a score of 5–4 in twelve innings. Christian Bullock, Michigan's left fielder, dropped a ball most of us thought we could catch. He certainly should have caught it. This player is excellent and had probably never dropped a ball like that in his life. But he allowed UCLA to win game two. I woke up in the middle of the night wondering if Bullock could sleep after that game—I certainly couldn't!

On Sunday, Ian drove me to UCLA's Jackie Robinson Stadium. I was not optimistic about Michigan's chances. But Ian was driving, and I love Michigan. Good deal! I learned a lot about the Tesla on the way to the stadium. The car is fantastic, but the crowd was cruel. When Christian Bullock went to bat, the UCLA chants began: "Butterfingers, butterfingers!" One guy yelled, "Bullock, if you could catch, this series would be over by now!" Others proclaimed Bullock to be UCLA's most valuable player.

Bullock walked and stole second base. Later in the game, he hit a double and then a triple. Now I know there is a god. But the game was not over.

With two outs late in the game, a Michigan player tried to steal second base and was called out. The umpires stopped the game to check the video. After a minute or so, the umpire gave the safe signal, and the Michigan team returned to the field to continue the inning. Baseball has changed since I watched Willie Mays play.

The game had everything. I saw Michigan's right fielder throw a ball from the outfield to home so the catcher could tag a UCLA runner out at the plate.

Many say baseball is like life itself. I believe this. It's never over until it is over, as accomplished philosopher Yogi Berra informed us. Michigan won. We went to the College World Series. Like I said, there is a god.

Ian Lazarus.

Paul Buck and Reva Wright: Lesson No. 1

The Red Cross was a wonderful place to meet wonderful people. I met Paul Buck around 1998. He was the CFO of the Southern California Region of the American Red Cross (ARC) Blood Services. Paul was born in Switzerland and went to a Jesuit high school in Rhodesia. His parents were missionaries. His wife, Reva, was born in Oklahoma and had overseen projects in India and other locations for Deloitte & Touche, the largest multinational professional services network in the world. We influenced each other's lives.

One of my favorite stories about Paul and Reva concerns their frequent trips to Europe, especially Switzerland. Paul traveled a lot for the ARC and rapidly accumulated frequent-flier miles. He once flew to Europe just to hand-deliver bone marrow the ARC had collected for a transplant recipient. Of course, Paul traveled coach, and the ARC paid for his ticket. But now he was taking his princess to Switzerland in coach using miles for a free ticket.

Though it was none of my business, I objected to this plan. I argued they should use those hard-earned miles to upgrade to first class and start the vacation at LAX before takeoff rather than upon landing in Switzerland. Reva saw the beauty in this plan. Paul did not.

Paul is frugal, a trait that served him well in many aspects of life if you can look past his wedding date. He married Reva on February 29. I never heard of anyone marrying on Leap Day. He reasoned that by marrying on February 29, he would only be buying an anniversary gift once every four years, allowing great cost-effectiveness. But Paul confessed that he had erred. His plan proved noneffective, unromantic, and a test of Paul's financial values.

Reva insisted (as she should have) on some annual recognition of their anniversary. February 28 would do in nonleap years. However, on February 29, annual recognition was inadequate. Something extraordinary was required when Leap Day arrived. Paul's frugal approach backfired. He must behave like all married men in three out of four years. But on Leap Day, he pays dearly. Paul learns like most of us—by experience.

I introduced Paul and Reva to first-class airline travel. Reva, CEO of the marriage, immediately embraced my plan for traveling to Europe only in a first-class cabin. If it weren't for me, Paul would have been able to retire about a decade earlier than he planned.

In return for my insight concerning air travel, Reva straightened out my life in regard to protecting one's home. I bought a home in La Jolla on Vallecitos in 1978. Since then, the home has been burglarized twice, once around 1987 and again in 2008. After the 2008 burglary on Christmas Eve, a police officer encouraged me to purchase a gun. That surprised me. After he took his report, I was told I would be contacted by an investigator. The investigator also asked if I owned a gun. I said no because I am under the impression that guns are associated with more "friendly fire" at home than the apprehension of burglars.

I told Reva the investigator said that if I was unfamiliar with guns, I should get a .22-caliber pistol because beginners find them easier to handle. Reva had a look of horror and disgust. All she could say was, "I don't want to annoy the guy; I want to kill him." That caught me off guard. Then I remembered: Reva was from Oklahoma. It all made sense.

Paul should be more careful about decisions that involve his marriage.

Paul Buck and Reva Wright: Lesson No. 2

Paul and Reva met in Los Angeles in 1985. This is not your usual couple. Reva left Oklahoma City for LA. Paul left Cape Town, South Africa, for LA. Then destiny took over.

Their story is unusual to a guy born and raised in New York City, who believed that after NYC, all the rest of the world is Bridgeport. If you just asked "What's Bridgeport?" I would say, "Exactly!"

Paul and Reva are citizens of Switzerland. Reva has dual citizenship. It was easy for Paul to be a Swiss citizen; his family is Swiss, and he was born there. But Reva hails from Oklahoma, not Bridgeport.

Paul and Reva. Photo courtesy of Paul Buck.

You just don't mess with her. The Swiss would have to deal with her. And they did.

Reva and Paul went to the Swiss consulate for Reva's final examination on becoming a citizen. I know a little of the truth, and I'll add my imagination. Reva was handling the oral portion of the examination well until the examiner asked her to name Switzerland's most valuable export. The answer is technology, and I suspect the Swiss are proud of it. But Reva was stumped. She studied for the finals, but this was not one of those study questions. She replied, "Chocolate."

This answer would probably sink the average applicant for citizenship. But Reva's demeanor is one of confidence and commitment. She turned the exam around and asked the examiner how often he had been to Carnival in Lucerne (the Luzerner Fasnacht is a notable festival in central Switzerland). The examiner was put on the spot and had to admit that he had never attended. "We go almost every year, so how Swiss are you?" Reva demanded. That was enough to embarrass the examiner and to welcome her to Switzerland. She now has her Swiss passport.

But the adventurer is not from Oklahoma. It's the Swiss native, Jesuit-educated-in-Africa Paul Buck whose exploits rival the romance of hiking the 2,180-mile Appalachian Trail. Paul Buck did the real thing while Martin Sheen superbly acted the part.

See the movie *The Way*. It is about an American father who goes to France to retrieve the body of his estranged son. The father, played by Sheen, resolves to walk Spain's Camino de Santiago de Compostela to better understand his son's life and his own. The Camino ultimately terminates on the shore of Galicia at Cape Finisterre (Latin for "land's end"). The scallop shell is the symbol of the pilgrimage.

The walk traditionally starts from a pilgrim's front door anywhere in Europe. However, modern pilgrims commonly start in Saint-Jean-Pied-de-Port in the foothills of the French Pyrenees and take about thirty-five days to reach Santiago de Compostela in Spain (ten to fourteen miles per day). This route, known as the Camino Français, is about 800 kilometers, or 500 miles. Those who continue to Finisterre add forty-five miles to the route. Paul, being Swiss, felt he needed to start from Geneva, Switzerland, which made the Camino 1,200 miles long. Twenty years ago, I would have loved this adventure. Even now it sounds enticing, although a back injury on July 7, 2017, has changed my perspective on adventure. But that is another story, and Paul says that if one can walk four miles, one can ultimately do the Camino. So never say never.

Paul did the walk from Geneva to Finisterre and subsequently used an ancient route, the Via Francigena, to make his way from London to Rome. What is going on here? I think I know. Paul's adventure is a statement of his values. What does one value in life? Religion? Family? Money? Glory? Montaigne would be disappointed if you chose one of these. In his essay "Of Solitude," Montaigne says, "Solitude seems to me more appropriate and reasonable for those who have given to the world their most active and flourishing years. . . . We have lived enough for others; let us live at least this remaining bit of life for ourselves."[*]

---

[*] Michel de Montaigne, "Of Solitude," in *The Complete Essays of Montaigne*, trans. Donald M. Frame (Palo Alto, CA: Stanford University Press, 1958).

Paul Buck at the zero-kilometer marker on the Camino de Santiago de Compostela. Photo courtesy of Paul Buck.

The lesson here is that life is to be experienced. Money has value insomuch as it provides an opportunity for experience. And sometimes Paul just needs to treat Reva to first class.

Bill Fileti

As I mentioned in my essay "On My Obsession with Michigan Football," I need to be in Michigan Stadium next to more than one hundred thousand fans even though I would have a better view at home. The live environment has a spiritual effect on me. Yet the experience is most intense when I am alone with one hundred thousand fanatics. I prefer not to invite a friend.

When you ask someone to join you at a game, a reasonable person expects to engage in some conversation. The talk may be about politics, business, or a great experience one wishes to share. This kind of conversation fascinates me, but not when I'm in Michigan Stadium.

A year or two after the stadium was renovated in 2010, I took my place in Section 417, Row 1, Seat 13 for the start of a new season. Next to me was a tall, calm man who seemed to be about fifty or fifty-five years old. He appeared pensive, and I had been wondering what he was thinking when his focus intensified as the public address announcer proclaimed, "Band, take the field."

I don't know why tears come to my eyes when I hear those words at the first home game of the season. But to my shock, I thought I saw the same tears in this guy's eyes.

I don't remember if Bill was with his wife, Cecilia, when I first observed him. I do remember that Eric, his older son who lived in Ann Arbor, attended a few games later in the year. Their younger son, Owen, lives in Los Angeles and rarely gets back to Ann Arbor. It would be several years before I would meet Owen and wife, Kristina. On this particular day, I was alone with a stranger who could not possibly know he was being observed with admiration.

It is difficult to understand what inspires or motivates an individual. Why did I want to get to know this guy? I realized I had to break my rule of solitude when a Michigan hype video played on the screen. Looking at Bill during the video, I thought I saw myself in the mirror—only this image was a handsome man of about six foot two.

I said nothing on that day. But I went back to our Ann Arbor condo and told Dale I saw myself in a guy who was sitting next to me. Dale asked what he was like, but I didn't know because I hadn't spoken to him.

When I broke the solitude rule, I discovered an amazing family. They had no incentive to make any impression on me. They were naturally comfortable. I started to share a little about myself. I smile when I think I was sharing a new experience with the Fileti family when I explained my love of haute cuisine. When I mentioned a restaurant I thought Bill and Cecilia should try, Cecilia told me about the chef and dinner parties and fundraisers the Fileti family supported. The family that was randomly assigned to sit next to me were Ann Arbor movers and shakers.

It was not just Michigan football and dining we had in common. The romantic in Bill surfaced when John Will and I happened to walk by Gratzi, an Italian restaurant in Ann Arbor. I noticed Bill and Cecilia sitting by the window overlooking Main Street, and they waved to us to indicate they had places for us at the table! We joined the family, and I learned about romance.

Bill said he had just invited Cecilia to Paris for dinner on Valentine's Day. That is my definition of taking romance to a new level. Cecilia is a princess, and I give credit to her for realizing her regal status and to Bill for treating her accordingly.

Any princess is accustomed to having things her own way—sort of like in When Harry Met Sally, a movie by Rob Reiner. Cecilia explained that Bill got full credit for the thought, but it needed modification. I incredulously asked how it was possible to modify a dinner in Paris. Cecilia sincerely stated Paris is best in springtime. February is too cold, and the summer is too hot. That was the day I decided that whenever I thought I had a good idea, I would run it by Cecilia for confirmation.

In the stadium, Bill was a student of the game. On October 17, 2015, something happened that caused me to pray for a personal dose of Alzheimer's disease. Before a crucial fumble that resulted in a Michigan loss, I looked at Bill. He was shaking his head.

"Bill, what's wrong?" I asked.

"This punting formation is a bad idea," Bill said. "They will be coming at us with all they've got. We should run the ball."

He was right. And from that time onward, during crucial times in a game, I would ask Bill what he thought our next play should be.

I got an email from Cecilia on December 13, 2016, inviting me to meet Coach Jim Harbaugh during the last Michigan home practice before a bowl game. I was so excited I booked my flight immediately. It's interesting how priorities change as one ages. There was a time I would have said that I couldn't get away from work. In reality, I had an exaggerated sense of importance regarding my work. The work always gets done. My priorities are healthier today.

Bill died of a brain tumor on April 22, 2017. It all happened so fast. When I woke up the day of the funeral, it was pouring rain. I have never heard rain that loud. But that is what humans do: we cry when we suffer the greatest loss of all. The weather was perfect.

The funeral did have a strange aspect. Such processions usually involve a motorcade of black vehicles, often led by limousines, like Lincoln Town Cars or Cadillacs. Several ambulances led Bill's funeral. My first thought was, *It's too late for that.*

That's because I didn't know everything about Bill yet. I knew he was a Michigan man and certainly a family man. Then I found out that Bill Fileti was a game changer. As a leader and executive administrator, he established one of the largest multispecialty medical groups in Michigan, with over five hundred physicians and five hundred thousand patients being served today. As a system thinker, Bill recognized that a community needs emergency services for its patients. In the late 1970s and early 1980s, several ambulance companies failed to serve the Ann Arbor community. They were poorly managed. Bill and his team used superb management skills to establish

Bill in the Big House.

Bill Fileti, fourth from left, and his family next to Michigan head coach
Jim Harbaugh in December 2016. It was an honor for me to join them.

the Huron Valley Ambulance (HVA) company. The HVA ambulances
at the funeral were there to say thank you.

When the day was over and I got back to the condo, I looked
up at the scoreboard that is visible from my living room window.
Cecilia had arranged to creatively utilize the Michigan Stadium scoreboard. Bill's image filled the screen. He was up there with the best.

Arthur J. Silvergleid and Margaret Anderson-Silvergleid

Art and Peggy came into my life in the 1980s. They both had
careers in transfusion medicine and blood banking in California
before retiring to St. Petersburg, Florida. Both Dale and Peggy have
special credentials designated as MT (ASCP) SBB—that is, medical
technologist with specialty in blood banking. Art is an internist, and

I am a pathologist. It is not surprising that our common interests brought us together.

Art is my lifetime coach and mentor. Several times when I've been preparing for a talk at a national meeting, he has provided me with the encouragement to finish the job. Over thirty years ago, Art gave a lecture on the indications for platelet transfusion. I marveled at the construction of the talk, which covered the safety issues of donor recruitment, collection of blood products, storage, distribution, and transfusion of the patient. The logical sequence of the discussion served as a template for all my efforts to provide continuing medical education to my medical staff.

Yet Art's mentoring went beyond professionalism. If you will accept the hypothetical construct of Freud's ego, superego, and id, Art was my superego. Whenever I had impetuous ideas, he tried to calm my id. At times, his efforts didn't work. I got burned and learned from experience.

It is a true friend who takes the time to correct the misdirected efforts of another. One could say that the harder the message is to deliver, the closer the friend who tells it.

Peggy and Art make a striking couple—*Esquire* or *Glamour* magazine striking. Yet Peggy is tough—really tough. When Peggy makes up her mind, Dale and I almost immediately agree. Sometimes Art doesn't. What ensues then is almost out of *Who's Afraid of Virginia Woolf?* The screen chemistry of Elizabeth Taylor and Richard Burton reminds me of Art and Peggy. The strange part of witnessing this experience is that after a few minutes of these hotly contested affairs, I lose track of what the argument is about.

During episodes of altercation, Peggy always looks assured. Art looks frustrated. Then it all dies down. My conclusion is that Peggy is so good in bed that Art has unconsciously (or maybe consciously) reasoned that in the balance of life, the scales tip toward the bedroom. I tell myself that story because that is how I think.

Art opened a surprising chapter in my life when he introduced me to the world of wine. Up until the 1980s, my experience with wine did not extend beyond Ripple or Swiss Colony. One night, we invited Art and Peggy for dinner, and they brought a bottle of Jordan and a bottle of Silver Oak—cabernet sauvignon vintages from the 1980s.

Arthur Silvergleid and Margaret Anderson-Silvergleid in the 1990s.

Unlike Jordan, Silver Oak only produced cabernet, and it sold license plate frames that read, "Life is a Cabernet."

When I took the two bottles from Art, I thought it was a nice gesture. But when Art removed the cork from the Silver Oak, it stopped me in my tracks. That aroma changed my annual liquor budget for the rest of my life. I studied and drank a lot of wine. I started talking about wine too much. There is a saying attributed to Fran Lebowitz that kept me grounded: "Great people talk about ideas, average people talk about things, and small people talk about wine."

Nonetheless, as I will explain in the essay titled "Fine Dining in New York City," my interest in wine was more than two standard deviations out. Art is more than a physician and enologist. He is a catalyst for exploring new experiences.

We explored the Mediterranean and the Baltic Seas together. This was when we learned how different two couples could be. Art and Peggy are out of bed at dawn and raring to go. They get maximum value from a cruise, fully exploring every port we visit. As for me, I will do all I can to avoid setting an alarm at bedtime. In Marseille, Art and Peggy saw the entire town. By the time Dale and I were out of bed, only the afternoon remained. I love that pace.

When all four of us were in China in 2004, our Chinese guide marveled at Art and Peggy holding hands in public. This natural display of affection was unnatural in China. So when spouses were separated for a banquet dinner, the only reason Peggy didn't sit with Art was her inability to communicate in Chinese. Otherwise, the Chinese culture would have changed that night.

We all have some memories that do not dim with time. Though we physically change as we age, I continue to see Art and Peggy as they were in 1993. That year, Art was the president of our professional organization (the AABB) and Peggy was its first lady. Just like John Travolta (as Danny Zuko) and Olivia Newton-John (as Sandy) in the movie Grease, Art and Peggy had the "spotlight" dance at the annual AABB banquet. They were front and center—where they belonged.

Michael Orlando, MD, PhD

If Arthur Silvergleid is my superego, Michael Orlando is my id. His impetuous thoughts and acts have entertained me for a lifetime. He was born in Altoona, Pennsylvania, and raised as an Italian Catholic. We met as pathology residents at the National Institutes of Health in Bethesda, Maryland.

For me, the responsibilities of a resident were demanding and far-reaching. I needed to work more than sixty hours a week to accomplish what others could do in far less time. But Michael was so fast and driven that he moonlighted as an emergency room doctor while I was catching my breath and sleeping most nights. In those years, I was not a long-range planner. My only goal was to master the field of surgical pathology. Michael was two steps ahead, not only doing what was expected of him, but planning his next career move—to be the pathologist and medical director of the laboratory at Fauquier Hospital in Warrenton, Virginia, where he covered the emergency room.

Michael's hobby is entertainment. He sang in community theater and tried his voice in an operetta. Another part of his personality is openly lusting for almost every girl who passes by. His craving for the opposite sex is visible to the onlooker, and in all fairness, the women seemed captivated by him. At the top of my career, in the 1990s and later, I worked in a blood bank with a nurse manager, Teresa DeShields. When she listened to me talk about Art Silvergleid and Michael Orlando, she smiled and said Dr. Silvergleid was the angel on my shoulder. On the other shoulder was Michael Orlando, the devil in disguise.

Of course, I don't think of Michael as evil in any way. He is a loving father and now grandfather. Yet he has struggled all his life with temp-tation. Often, I imagined he would lose the battle and be proud of it.

Michael survives from day to day with lifelong canine companions. Sophie and Ollie, Wheaton terriers, were his roommates for fifteen years. Wheaton terriers, characterized by grace and strength, origi-nally were bred in Ireland to hunt and protect farms. Small rodents do not survive an encounter with these dogs, and Michael's dogs lived up to this reputation. A groundhog in Davidson, North Carolina, made the mistake of wandering onto Michael's property. Groundhogs in well-developed areas are nearly free of predators, Wikipedia says, and they live about three years in the wild. The Wheatons, the more aggressive Sophie and her pal Ollie, were responsible for lowering the average age of groundhogs in Davidson, North Carolina.

Michael's creativity led him to develop a syllabus for an undergraduate- and graduate-level course he called From Matter to Metaphysics. He spoke to a Jesuit priest who headed the Department of Biology at Georgetown University who expressed interest and planned to offer the course for credit. But Michael related that the proposal did not survive an encounter with human behavior and jealousy. While the value of this unique course was acknowledged by the head of the department, the faculty did not cherish it. Michael did not have an appointment on the faculty of a university. Permitting him to teach a course in which students earned credits toward a baccalaureate degree was a dangerous precedent in the opinion of the faculty, and they would have none of it. And they accomplished their goal.

As a man now in his late seventies, Michael is retired and writing a novel. He is cursed with thoughts of the hereafter. He speaks of concepts like "genetic drag," which may very well have baffled Watson and Crick. He once told me there was a time in his early years when he considered the priesthood. Such a consideration must have lasted a millisecond after the concept of celibacy was explained.

Today Michael wonders about the soul. Is there a part of you, your spirit or essence, that lives on after death? I am blessed in that these thoughts never enter my mind. Somehow, I can live with the discrepant belief that it's all over when it's over and still feel a responsibility to contribute while I am here. Try your best to make a positive difference knowing full well that when it's over, there will be no one to say, "Good job." There will be no final judgment day. I'm OK with that. Michael is not. My view would probably work out better for Michael.

To fully appreciate the sense of Michael's personality, I include two emails and one handwritten letter. First, I share my email communications that preceded Michael's email replies. The letter is vintage Michael and was not prompted by any action on my part.

My email to Michael in 2011:

On Sunday, while watching TV interviews of 911, I got most depressed thinking of Jessica. My loss is different than the families of 911, but no less painful. It all started recurring again before I went to sleep. Then I was comforted by what you said to me 10 years ago. You spoke of "Vincent (Starry Starry Night)" sung by Don McLean. No words have comforted me more than these:

> But, I could have told you, Vincent
> This world was never meant for one
> As beautiful as you.

Michael's email reply in 2011:

Hi Jerry,

I am sorry that you had and continue to suffer the pain of your tragic loss. The irony of being human is that we are rewarded for having consciousness with the joy of good experiences, and then the abject misery of losing what we love, often laced with a heaping dose of guilt. Fortunately, we do not see this coming when we are young, but by the time we reach complete maturity, we begin to dread the loss of our attachments even more than our own senescence and death. The most important reason that humans cling to the notion of an eternal God is hope that some part of our consciousness will persist and allow us to meet up with those things we lost in life. In a life full of delusion and pain, why not have the most meaningful delusion of all. Sometimes, on a starry moonlit night, I look to the heavens, and imagine I am communicating with those who have gone before me. Hopefully, you are past the paralyzing state of acute grief, and can open your soul to the wonders of the universe, and the consolation of knowing that there is a small but definite possibility that something better is coming. Evil, of which I consider loss to be a prime example, is a by-product of the struggle to evolve. We are asked to make many sacrifices on behalf of the struggle. At least, we can believe that it is for a good cause. Montaigne has an essay on sadness in which he urges us not to indulge the low feeling for it makes us unhappy and weak. Good advice, difficult to do. We should talk soon! Thanks for reminding me of "Vincent." I will go to u-tube [*sic*] right now and play it for all of us.

Mike

Another email I sent to Michael seeking to better understand myself, this one in 2016:

Trouble sleeping tonight. So I re-watched Clint Eastwood's movie *Gran Torino*. I'd like to know why I cry at the end. I see it coming but it still brings tears to my eyes.

> Gentle now a tender breeze blows
> Whispers through the Gran Torino
> Whistling another tired song
> Engines hum and better dreams grow
> Heart locked in a Gran Torino
> It beats a lonely rhythm
> All night long
> It beats a lonely rhythm
> All night long
> It beats a lonely rhythm
> All night long

Michael's reply to my email:

Hi Jerry,

Steve Hajdu used to say that the American 8-cylinder engines in the proper car such as a Gran Torino were so good that you could get in and drive from coast to coast only stopping for gas.

I suspect you are crying because you sense that the era when things were meant to work hard, perform well, and last forever is gone from our lives. More importantly, and I think about this very often, when you remember the past, you miss the experiences, people, and stability; but most of all, you are grieving for the loss of your youth, during which time all of those seemingly wonderful things were occurring (and it did not concern you that the Gran Torino had a reputation for rusting out).

As I have grown older, more irrelevant, and almost completely devoid of "new" and exhilarating experiences, my thoughts turn to the fun of a new encounter with a fresh and sexual young woman. This, while driving my 1966 Trans Am, playing racquet ball, and later playing the McIntosh stereo. Last week I saw a new dark blue BMW M6 convertible in a parking lot. It had the best looking dark red leather interior I have ever seen. I actually stood and dreamed about being behind the wheel driving at 100 mph going nowhere. Then, reality crept in, and I walked away. For money, I could have any of those things, though the energy and enthusiasm I could bring to the party would be sorely lacking, and I would end up feeling ashamed. The only comfort I have is in saying we all spent our youth pursuing, and believing in dreams; and living those dreams gave us great pleasure. I can still dream about dreaming.

It is getting harder to look to the future for pleasure, and so, late at night when we cannot sleep, we either find a modicum of comfort in our memories, or distract ourselves by watching movies such as *Gran Torino*, and sob for the loss of a time we can never recapture. Loss, real or imagined, is the most serious of the obstacles that impede human happiness. As we grow older, the only antidote for loss is to concentrate on the little personal joys of daily life, and our dependable old memories. This is when Oscar Wilde's statement "Living well is the best revenge" makes the most sense; although it is very important to define *well* for ourselves.

Traveling now beats a lonely rhythm for me. Years ago, no matter how hard the travel, I would wake up to the possibility of a new adventure. Now, I wake up and even more acutely feel the loss of those things I value so much in my narrow existence. I am thankful to have experienced life with consciousness. When the old body seems to be calling us toward the big sleep, the qualities of consciousness (imagination, memory, thought, analysis) all can be used to make life interesting and tolerable.

I have an old movie for you to try: It's called *Wrestling with Ernest Hemingway* and stars Robert Duvall and Richard Harris. Tell me what you think!

Mike

The beauty of Michael's reply persuaded me that his insight needed to be shared. I sent it to Art Silvergleid. Art wrote back with even more wisdom. Life improves immeasurably when your friends are sages. Art's thoughts:

I guess it comes down to how you look at it. I value nostalgia; in fact, I treasure nostalgia. I love to let it come over me in waves so that I can feel it, in the moment, more intensely. I always get nostalgic when I am on the last chair lift of the last day of my annual Boys' ski week, remembering how much I love the experience, the shared memories over 50 years, and the friendship behind it, and wondering whether it will ever happen again, or just be consigned to the dust bin of my memory. I get nostalgic when I remember my days at the U of R and the intense relationships with gals and guys, many of whom have recently passed away, and what impact they had on my life. I get nostalgic thinking about celebrating my 70th birthday both in Stockholm, at the start of an incredible journey around the Baltic Sea, and on a snowy night in NYC at the Met.

The arc of our lives, as Michael points out, has crested, no doubt. Beautiful young women at the grocery store no longer look at me with interest, or flirt with me; they say "sir" and ask if they can help me carry my groceries. I accept that, not that I would ever stop looking. I've had a love of my life with one of the most beautiful women I've ever known; that memory sustains me, since I have neither the resources, nor interest, to follow in Hugh Hefner's footsteps.

While nostalgia is healthy, I believe, a lack of enthusiasm for what lies ahead is not; that's where the sadness comes. There are still goals to reach: places to visit, people to meet, shooting my age on a golf course, reminiscing with longtime friends, sharing a great meal or better bottle of wine, watching the next generation take their place and reach their destiny, aging gracefully, but well. I feel for Michael and wish his outlook could be a mixture of nostalgia and anticipation; lack of the latter lets the sadness in.

Perhaps the reason I offer these email exchanges is a desire for some semblance of immortality. Not just for me but for my friends. This reminds me of words I attribute to Woody Allen. The story goes that someone told Woody that he had achieved immortality through his movies. He said he didn't want to achieve immortality through his movies; he wanted to achieve immortality by not dying.

And finally, that letter from Michael that seemingly appeared out of the blue circa 1980:

Dear Jerry & Dale,

Thank you for the Christmas card and the picture of the children. They are good looking kids and appear to be thriving in the California environment.

We sent no Christmas cards this year but decided instead to save the communication for times when the spirit (our spirits) might need enriching. So tonight, just two weeks past the holiday season I am feeling lonely despite the typical family chaos. It's a good time to write. I have finally achieved success.

I now own or partially own (in conjunction with 17 banks) over 12,000 objects which themselves can be broken down into 320,000 functional parts of which 5% are either broken or in need of maintenance at any one time; each requiring that either I fix it or call in some ass who upon seeing how much I own, right before my eyes mutates into a Marxist and proceeds to distribute my "wealth" to the heroic working class. Each of these encounters leaves me feeling guilty for being so lucky to own so much. So not wishing to feel the pangs of guilt I have begun avoiding these encounters. Hence, my entire life is now dedicated to the maintenance of things which I no longer have time to enjoy.

I have a recurring nightmare in which I am pompously driving along in my BMW when I am suddenly pulled off the road by two Japanese policemen driving a 62-inch Sony television set. They accuse me of fraud in that my Blaupunkt radio is really made in Japan and they confiscate it. I race home to tell my wife the horrible news only to find her in bed with Ron Elin who is wearing my Christian Dior bathrobe, drinking my 1957 Dom Perignon and smoking my best Havana cigar while watching videotape replays [of himself giving a Nobel Prize acceptance speech for his work with Limulus crabs in the Chesapeake Bay] on my fully digital solid state, micro-computerized, 2000 chip, 4000 bit Nakamichi audio cassette machine. I shoot both of them and feel properly vindicated. The scene shifts to my courtroom trial, which is being held in Argentina where no man has ever been convicted for a crime of passion where his wife was involved.

Things seem to be going my way when I look at the crowd and see Bo Derek in the first row gently scribing little circles on her exposed creamy thigh with a moist index finger. She winks. My heart is racing, and I turn to face the jury.

Cos Berard, Mark Zweig, Magda, Alan Rabson, Jimmy Carter, Bernie Kasten, Barry Cook, my father, Ruth Rabson, Arnold Rabson, an IRS agent, Attila the Hun

The Verdict: Guilty

The sentence is to personally perform the autopsies on every illegal alien who enters New York City for the next 50 years.

I awake in a cold sweat just glad to be alive in my warm bed with my wife who is purring softly in my ear. A quick check on the children and they are fine. I riffle through the desk and see the bank statements are marked paid. Finally, I streak to the garage, fling open the door, and there sits my angry, nothing ever breaks,

8-cylinder, 10 mpg, bad assed, made in Detroit Trans Am. By God, everything's going to be OK!!

The Orlando's are fine. It is a heavy time of year here in the post Christmas, gray, frigid almost northeast. When your work focuses on disease, dying and death, we sometimes have to remember that the daffodils will once again bloom in springtime.

Despite everything that I have, and God knows there is plenty to be thankful for, I do sometimes feel lonely. It's the loneliness that comes from always being the one who sleeps closest to the door. It's hearing the little boy say, "Let me get in the middle" and wishing for a moment that you could trade places with him. It's knowing that you have scored your last touchdown, Elvis was a pervert, Santa doesn't exist, presidents cheat, nuns shit, and Hayley Mills is middle aged that makes me lonely—sometimes.

Here is hoping that we can get together soon.

Warm regards,
Michael

I have included images of Michael's note. I had affixed it to a wall so that I might be reminded often of its insight, but forty years of sunlight have done some damage. Even if the words are faded, the sentiment remains strong:

Dear Jerry & Dale,

Thank you for the christmas card and the picture of the children. They are good looking kids and appear to be thriving in the California environment.

We sent no christmas cards this year but decided instead to save the communication for times when the spirit (our spirits) might need enriching. So tonight, just two weeks past the holiday season I am feeling lonely despite the typical family chaos. It's a good time to write. I have finally achieved success.

I now own or partially own (in conjunction with 17 banks) over 12,000 objects which themselves can be broken down into 320,000 functional parts of which 5% are either broken or in need of maintenance at any one time; each requiring that either I fix it or call in some ass who upon seeing how much I own, right before my eyes mutates into a Marxist and proceeds to distribute my "wealth" to the heroic working class. Each of these encounters leaves me feeling guilty for being so lucky to own so much. So not wishing to feel the pangs of guilt I have begun avoiding these encounters. Hence, my entire life is now dedicated to the maintenance of things which I no longer have time to enjoy.

over

... I am suddenly rattled off to ... by two Japanese ... observers on B&y television set. They accuse me of fraud in that my Blaupunkt was ... made in Japan and they don't want it. I race home to tell my wife the terrible news only to find her in bed with Don Chu who is wearing my Christian Dior bathrobe, drinking my 1957 Dom Perignon and smoking my best Havana cigar while watching ... we ... (of himself giving a Nobel prize acceptance speech for his work with ... crabs in the Chesapeake Bay) on my fully digital, solid state, micro computerized, 2000 chip, 1000 bit Nakamichi audio cassette machine. I shoot both of them and feel properly vindicated. The scene shifts to my court room of veal which is being held in Argentina where no man has ever been convicted for a crime of passion where his wife was involved.

Things seem to be going my way when I look at the crowd and see Bo Derek in the first row gently scribing little circles on her exposed creamy thigh with a moist index finger. She winks. My heart is racing and ...

The ...

The ...

I topple through the ... as ...
statements are ... court. Finally I stand in
the garage, peering over the door and there, to my
... nothing was broken. Remember ... money, had well
made in Detroit ... By God, everything's
going to be OK !!

The Oriental's are ... It's a heavy
time of year here ... the poor Christmas ; my ,
frozen almost northeast. When your work
focuses on disease, dying and death it's sometimes
hard to remember that the daffodils will once
again bloom in springtime.

Despite everything that we have and God knows
there is plenty to be thankful for, I do
sometimes feel lonely. It's the loneliness that

comes from always being the one who sleeps
closest to the door. It's hearing the little boy
say "let me get in the middle" and wishing
for a moment that you could trade places with
him. It's realizing that there will never again
be a friend who isn't going to move away so
far that you can't sit across the table from him.
It's knowing that you have scored your last
touchdown, Elvis was a pervert, Santa doesn't exist,
Presidents cheat, Nuns shit and Harley Mills is
middle aged that makes me lonely—sometimes.
Here's hoping that we can get together soon.

Warm regards.

Michael

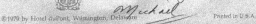

Dr. Michael Orlando with his Wheaton terriers.

Teresa Deshields, left, described Dr. Silvergleid as the angel on my right shoulder and Dr. Orlando as the devil on my left shoulder. Nurse Kris Koehler, right, worked with me in the blood bank.

Michael Orlando and me.

TWELVE

Personal

The Thank-You Card

M ichael Covert had something about him that is inspiring. I needed to be regularly dosed with Michael.

In 2003, Michael was selected by the board of directors of Palomar Health as the new CEO. He remained our CEO for over ten years before being offered a job as CEO of St. Luke's Health in Houston and then becoming senior vice president of operations at Denver-based Catholic Healthcare Initiatives in 2014. Many members of the medical staff described Michael as charismatic. He offered me my first job in quality as the newly appointed associate chief medical quality officer (ACMQO).

One of my responsibilities as ACMQO was to provide all new employees with an introduction to our quality and safety program at an orientation. I included a discussion of the culture transformation necessary to achieve high reliability at the orientations, which were conducted once or twice a month. After I spoke, Michael would address the new employees on our vision, mission, and values. I often joked that I warmed up the crowd for Michael. But I attended his talk every four to six months even though the content did not change. I needed a regular dose of Michael because his delivery was uplifting.

I shared a story with Michael one day about one of our clinical laboratory scientists, Kenneth Broeckel, who alerted me to an angry orthopedic surgeon. I got Ken's call on a Saturday around 7:00 p.m. He told me that the orthopedic surgeon was upset about a delay in his order for an immediate prothrombin time (PT), a type of blood test. Ken told me the surgeon would not let him explain what happened. Instead, the doctor cursed at the medical technologist and shouted, "I will get to Dr. Kolins about this!"

The key part of the story is that Ken Broeckel explained to me that the doctor had inadvertently ordered the blood draw to take place the next morning, even though he needed the results immediately. I had the ammunition I needed thanks to Ken's conscientious work in getting me that information quickly. I was ready for the orthopedic surgeon. When he called, I even exhibited a little emotional intelligence by reassuring him that his reputation for high quality was well known. I started with a compliment. Then I explained he had ordered the test for tomorrow morning. There was silence on the phone for several seconds. Then the doctor said, "Maybe I need more training on the computer." I said that could be arranged.

After relating this story to our CEO, he asked me if I sent Ken a thank-you card. I said I hadn't, and then I made a crucial mistake. "Michael, you are correct," I said. "It only takes a minute to type a thank-you and hit the send button."

"Dr. Kolins, you don't listen," he replied. "I said a 'thank-you card.' You take a pen, paper, envelope, and stamp. Write the three sentences, address the envelope, and mail it to Ken's home."

Many thoughts raced around in my head, but I decided not to share them, which represented another example of emotional intelligence. I say this because my thought was that I was not going to do it. That was just what my mother made me do after my bar mitzvah. If I had known about the thank-you requirement, I would have recommended that we not have a party.

Then it happened. About three months later, I got a thank-you card from an appreciative nurse. It moved me. I couldn't even throw the card in the wastepaper basket at the end of the week. I decided to pin it to the bulletin board.

It finally dawned on me that if I reacted to a thank-you card this way, I hadn't understood its power. I started to write them. The tool is so powerful that I began receiving thank-you cards for my thank-you cards—unbelievable!

I made a promise. I would never let myself write a thank-you card to a person who sent me a written thank-you because I sent them a thank-you card. That is too much.

But then I lost it when I received the following card from Mary Hart, an exercise physiologist:

Every once in a while in life, we are blessed with amazing surprises that cause us to smile from the inside out. That is how I felt the day I received your note regarding your visit to Cardiac Rehab. The fact that you would take the time to do such a nice thing meant so much! So I guess what I'm trying to say is, "Thank you for the thank you!" It was appreciated more than you can ever know. Sincerely, Mary

I broke my rule and wrote a thank-you card to Mary for thanking me for my original card. I needed to tell her how much she moved me. She made my day with her words.

This experience taught me that humans appreciate being appreciated. Some make the argument that thank-you cards are inappropriate because employees are simply doing what we hired them to do. But the thank-you card is more than just a show of appreciation; it is a powerful tool for cultural transformation. It changes behavior and attitudes, and that transforms the culture into one of compassion and high reliability.

The Motorcycle and the Department of Motor Vehicles

Have you ever watched Walt Disney's animated version of *The Wind in the Willows*? It's based on a novel by Kenneth Grahame first published in 1908. Disney released the DVD in 2009. It's the character Mr. Toad who intrigues me so. When Mr. Toad sees his first motor car, his eyes bug out like a Margaret Keane painting. That happened to me when I saw my first motorcycle.

Motorcycles were popular at the University of Michigan in the 1960s. Against good reason and with strong objections from my parents, I spent about $700 on a Honda S90 during my junior year. Pristine examples of this model can be tracked down on the internet today, though it was only produced from 1964 to 1969. As of this writing, the internet shows a current value of about $3,000. The engine was 89.6 cc (hence S90), and it had a four-speed transmission with chain drive. It could go sixty miles per hour and get ninety miles per gallon. My eyes bugged out when I saw these bikes around campus. I'm not a big guy, so the small size of the bike was perfect for me.

One Sunday after studying, I decided to take a short ride to the outskirts of Ann Arbor. The leaves were still on the trees, and the freedom of the ride was exhilarating. It is with a little embarrassment that I tell you I began to sing Dean Martin songs as I rode down Geddes Avenue. When I got to the song "The Door Is Still Open to My Heart," some insect flew into my throat. Perhaps it would be more accurate to say I flew into an insect. It took hours for that creature to dislodge. I guess I buried it in my pharyngeal mucosa. I stopped singing.

In the 1970s, the *Journal of the American Medical Association* published an article showing the risk of dying from a menu of events. One event listed was death from riding a motorcycle. That risk was one in fifty. I didn't know that in 1966. It was the Ann Arbor winter that taught me a lesson about riding and risk.

I was heading from the library to my apartment when I turned a corner and enjoyed a bit of speed. When I looked up, there was a patch of ice that caused me to panic and slam on the brakes. The back wheel swung around to the front. For an instant, it was like driving backward. The spin continued until the bike and I hit the ground.

A few students came running and helped me up. I only suffered a bruised ego and an impressively swollen elbow. I had previously invested in a high-end helmet that I always wore while riding. The helmet hit the ground, but I knew I was not seriously injured. That fall was the lesson. I knew then that the bike would not join me in Detroit when I started medical school in September 1968. I sold it in April 1968.

That was the end of my motorcycle experience until I got a call from Paul Buck, the adventurous guy who hiked the Camino de Santiago trail. I shouldn't have been surprised when Paul said, "We need to get motorcycle licenses."

You need an M1 license to ride a motorcycle on the streets and highways of California. This requires passing a written and practical test. I asked Paul how we could take the class without a motorcycle. Paul said students could rent them for class instruction, and the class was not taught on the public streets. It's was on a closed course for teaching. Wow, it was Mr. Toad again. Let's do it.

I drove up to Orange County in 2008 during the time of the housing crisis. Classes were all day Saturday and Sunday. Sunday afternoon was the final practical, so that day I retrieved my motorcycle for the last time and did the required figure eight for the instructor. A rectangle is drawn on the asphalt of the parking lot where the course was conducted. You must complete your figure eight within the white lines. The instructor watched me successfully complete this maneuver a few times in practice until he impatiently said, "Kolins, take the test. Stop these practice runs." When I took the test, one wheel nipped the white line of the rectangle. The instructor called me over and asked why I had done that. I didn't answer. He murmured something about how I was having too much fun and couldn't take the test again. He told me to return the motorcycle. I didn't tell him I had lost control unintentionally, and he passed me anyway.

Something happens when you become seventy. I think it has to do with adjusting to the realization that life must have an end. I get upset less often now. My attitude reminds me of the joke about the thirty-year-old guy in a Porsche who zooms in front of a Cadillac driven by a septuagenarian. The Porsche driver steals the old man's parking space. The speedster says, "See what you can do when you are young and fast?" The old guy drives his Cadillac into the Porsche and says, "See what you can do when you are old and don't give a damn?" Well, I'm there—except when it comes to renewing my driver's license.

I got a letter from the DMV in 2019 stating that my driver's license and my motorcycle license must be renewed, and I needed to be tested. "Damn it," I said. "That means I need to study. I don't want to lose that M1 designation. I needed to take both written tests again, not to mention the eye test, get the requisite photograph, and pay the $36 fee." That fee covers both the standard Class C license test for automobiles and the M1 test for motorcycles.

The last time I took a written test at the DMV, it really was a written test. You got a pencil, test paper with a few dozen questions, and a restricted, proctored area to complete the exam. This time there was just a row of computers, a barcode reader, a timer on the screen, and a proctor. Most questions had driving illustrations showing a situation you could encounter. You had to choose the best approach from the three options provided. Sometimes I just didn't know. For example, you are driving your motorcycle on a city street lined by parked cars. You are most likely to be injured by (1) an oncoming car, (2) a parked car leaving a parking space and entering the street, or (3) a door from a parked car that has just been opened by a driver attempting to exit his parked car. I got this one wrong. I answered no. 3, but the correct answer was no. 2.

Here is the part I didn't understand before I took the test. After you submitted each answer, you got an immediate reply stating whether your answer was right or wrong. When wrong, there was an obnoxious noise and a red X, but you got an explanation. You learned from your mistake. I failed the M1 test and passed the Class C test. I went to the proctor, who already knew this. I said I guessed God didn't want septuagenarians to drive motorcycles. She told me that I had paid for three tries. It's like baseball: three strikes and you're out. I told her I didn't want to drive back to the DMV for a second try. She said I only needed to wait five minutes for the system to reset.

On my second try, about a third of the questions had been on my first test. Many of them were the ones I got wrong the first time. I wondered if the system knew that. I'm not one to make the same mistake twice. I passed the M1 test and left the DMV ecstatic. It's surprising how easy it is to please a septuagenarian.

Fine Dining in New York City

Art Silvergleid is my closest friend and mentor in life and over my forty-year career in blood banking. It was my honor to take him and his wife, Peggy, to one of New York City's finest dining establishments on Art's seventieth birthday. That was in 2012.

It was a special evening because of the birthday milestone. And at that time, I wondered if I would make seventy myself. My health was good but not great. I had been treated with chemotherapy for chronic lymphocytic leukemia (CLL) in 2007, and on January 27, 2017, I was diagnosed with prostate cancer. Yet these malignancies were also diagnosed in my dad, who died just short of his eighty-fifth birthday of hospital-acquired complications. If that had occurred in California, the state Department of Public Health would have fined the hospital $50,000–$100,000. Since my dad had done just fine with his two malignancies, Art expected me to return to Daniel, the restaurant where we were celebrating, for my own seventieth birthday. He was right.

The evening was just as I hoped. Art and Peggy enjoyed the evening. Our thoughts involved wine. I have a few bottles of rare Burgundy wines, and at the time (2012), that included five bottles of Domaine de la Romanée-Conti. The vintage years were 2000–2004. Today, I still have some from 2001–3.

The value of these wines is astronomical, and I knew they would be. My knowledge was based on a lot of reading and an opportunity to buy a case from this vintner. Each case had just one bottle of the Romanée-Conti for that vintage. And each case cost about $2,000. I bought one case each year for five years in a row. The other eleven bottles were very good too.

I encourage the reader to learn the retail price of that one bottle of the Romanée-Conti included in each case. I use the Wine-Searcher application for price estimates. The bottles I still had as of 2019 retailed for about $20,000. Per bottle!

I have two favorite stories to share about these wines. The first occurred at the restaurant in La Jolla called George's at the Cove. It is a San Diego favorite but by no means a three-star Michelin. While dining there with Dale, a gentleman across from us heard me talking about three bottles of Romanée-Conti. He asked if I would be willing to sell them if they were in good condition.

Good condition! I store wines at fifty-seven degrees from the moment I purchase the bottle. These were in perfect condition.

He offered $20,000 in cash for three bottles. He thought I didn't know what I had. Nonetheless, I took his email address. Then I called Art.

Art listened attentively and then asked the most important question regarding the decision to keep or sell. "Imagine the $20,000 being placed in your hands after you give the gentleman the three bottles," Art said. "You now have $20,000 in cash. What is that thing you have always deprived yourself of because of the lack of cash? Here is your chance. What is that special thing you now can experience that you have been denied all your life?"

I told him I didn't think I had been denied anything. "Then you don't need the $20,000," Art said. I should do as I planned to do when I made the purchase: open the bottle and find out why people pay $20,000 just to taste that wine. Then Art said, "To make the experience special, you should invite me over to join you." And I did.

Story two involves a trip to NYC for my seventieth birthday. Art and Peggy couldn't join us, but I made it to seventy, so Dale and I would dine in NYC. I would return to my roots. My plan was to bring one of those bottles of Romanée-Conti (I had four left after Art and I shared a bottle) to the restaurant.

I called the restaurant, and they told me guests were prohibited from bringing their own wine into the restaurant, a three-star Michelin in 2017.

I was not to be intimidated. I explained that I was aware of the prohibition, but I understood that the owner made an exception for any guest who brings in a 2004 Romanée-Conti. At my suggestion, the restaurant staff member decided to check.

In two days, I got a call. The representative said it turned out I was right. Romanée-Conti 2004 was an exception to the rule, but I could not bring it with me when I arrived. I had to mail it in advance so other customers would not think the policy has changed.

Dale figured out how to mail a $20,000 bottle of wine across the country. On Wall Street in La Jolla, there is a storefront window with a sign that says "We ship olive oil anywhere." But the image was not a bottle of olive oil; it was a wine bottle.

We dined with Romanée-Conti in NYC.

Postscript: I was treated with proton therapy in 2019 for my prostate cancer. My PSA went from 9.3 to 0.4 in one year. The nadir was reached in about one year's time (July 2020). I feel cured—just like my dad after his prostate cancer was treated. More proof that Gregor Mendel knew his stuff even before DNA was discovered.

Some things you just don't sell, no matter how valuable. That includes my bottles of Romanée-Conti.

A Man's Got to Know His Limitations

Clint Eastwood made the line famous in his movie *Magnum Force*. I understand the concept. I turned back on Longs Peak with only about sixty minutes of additional hiking needed to reach the summit. Of course, I was with Jessica and deciding for both of us. But I knew our limitations. I also turned back from what would have been the highlight of a diving trip just ten minutes from the goal.

My interest in scuba diving occurred late in life. By February 14, 2013, I had completed the written examination, the free swim, and the scuba practical to become certified. I keep a diver's log and a record of my training. Since 2013, I have completed twenty-five dives, with the last one on August 3, 2018. That day was special, and I have labeled it "Turtle Soup with Jerry Kolins Day." I was surrounded by four Pacific green sea turtles, and as I was photographing one of them, my instructor took the photo of Turtle Soup.

In my seven years of scuba diving, I have photographed dozens of Hawaiian tropical fish, a whitetip reef shark, an octopus, the rare monk seal, a whitemouth moray eel and snowflake moray eel, trumpetfish, needlefish, and a male and a female harlequin shrimp. The male and female are often seen together, thus accounting for my image of the pair.

Scuba has opened a new world for me. Probably its most satisfying aspect is the complete silence you can enjoy at the bottom of the sea. Sometimes the only sound is your own breathing. Hearing is a sense that we cannot voluntarily turn off like we can vision. We can close our eyes, but we cannot close our ears—unless you scuba dive.

You can imagine my excitement when, on Wednesday morning, July 31, 2019, I went to the dive shop to book my first dive in over a year. The excitement was extinguished when I heard that the entire day was booked—not a single slot in a group dive or a private dive was available. Josh Cruz, at scheduling, said the shop had one opening for a scooter dive at 10:00 a.m. Thursday. I took it.

A scooter dive is a nickname for a diver propulsion vehicle (DPV). I chose this type of dive knowing that it would provide an even longer experience than scuba diving. There is about forty-five to sixty minutes of air in a tank. I use more oxygen when I am exerting myself, so the scooter permits ten to fifteen more minutes of fun and photography.

But I didn't want to waste Wednesday just because there would not be a dive. A snorkel in the coral reef would be a fun way to practice my photography.

The reef requires about a twenty-minute swim against a mild current to reach the mysteries the sea conceals. I am not a good enough swimmer to follow the fish along the ocean floor with a snorkel—even fifteen to twenty feet below. One needs to be careful. Your adventure can be ruined if the tide pushes you into the coral reef or, even worse, you accidentally touch the spines of a sea urchin. I stayed on the surface and took photos looking straight down. When I scuba dive, I often get below the subject or at least at the same depth. The photography is much more interesting with scuba—and I can breathe.

It shocked me how fast I began to huff and puff about twenty-five minutes into the swim toward the reef. I turned around and looked toward the shore. My goodness, I had drifted and swam a greater

A bit of Pacific sea turtle soup. My master scuba diving instructor, H. Jay Kuhlman, took this shot of me with these marvelous creatures off the coast of Wailea, Maui, on August 3, 2018.

distance than I appreciated. I had to ask myself whether to continue to the point of the reef that was my goal.

I know my limitations. It takes energy to return to safety. I wasn't sure if I had another twenty-five minutes in me. My thinking wasn't clear. I reasoned that because it took about twenty-five minutes to swim out to the coral, that's how long I would need to get back. But the current was with me on the return. It took about ten minutes.

I have no regrets. I needed more training and exercise to accomplish the swim I had planned. But my key goal was achieved. I returned safely. And tomorrow would be the scooter dive. I would have all the energy I needed for that one.

You Cannot Make an Asymptomatic Patient Feel Better

I have always thought of myself as relatively healthy—even though I was diagnosed with CLL in 2006 and was treated with six rounds of chemotherapy in 2007. I wasn't too worried at the time because a research scientist sent me articles showing that proper therapy would give me a 95 percent chance of being put into remission. Those are superb odds. I was cautiously optimistic.

The hematologist that prescribed the chemotherapy was anxious about giving me the high dose the new treatments were advocating. Then my closest friend, Arthur Silvergleid, an internist, made a crucial argument that changed my thinking and the course of treatment. He reasoned the 95 percent remission rate was only achieved with the high-dose regimen. He further argued that at my age of fifty-nine, I was in relatively good health, was not overweight, and had no other underlying serious medical conditions. He said go for the big dose. I did, and I have been in remission ever since.

Sure, as we get older, we get health issues. But nothing disturbed me more than a vacation to Maui in February 2020. I planned to bring the immediate family together, do a little scuba diving, and party (that's a code word for drinking).

I was walking to the concierge club, thinking it was time for a drink. It was after 4:00 p.m., and that is a reason to have a martini. Arthur Silvergleid explained to me why the Kolins family tradition considers 4:00 p.m. the bewitching hour. My dad, a product of the Great Depression, made a living in finance. His workday always ended when the New York Stock Exchange closed. Well, it's four o'clock somewhere.

While walking to the concierge club, I felt a pounding in my chest that was frightening. Doctors should not diagnose or treat themselves—especially pathologists. That was my first mistake. I have always assumed I would follow the same health path as my dad. I say that because I am convinced Gregor Mendel knew what he was talking about. My dad had CLL; I got CLL. Then my dad got prostate cancer; I got prostate cancer. He was cured with radiation; I was cured with proton therapy. There was only one family disease left for me to get—atrial fibrillation.

I incorrectly diagnosed atrial fibrillation with associated tachycardia (a heart rate of at least 100 beats per minute). My heart rate was over 160 beats per minute while I was gently walking to the club for a martini—not exactly a stressful moment.

In my return from Maui, I had an experience that pushed me from denial into the real world. While waiting to board the airplane, I passed out, falling over my roll-aboard. A passenger, who was also a physician, attended to me while I was unconscious. She told the paramedics no pulse was palpable for thirty seconds. There was a portable defibrillator (automated external defibrillator) attached to my chest. When I became conscious, I heard a mechanical voice from the device say, "Do not activate at this time." The sentence was repeated several times. I realized I needed help. But I said, "Let's listen to that machine!"

What happened to me next was a series of encounters with medicine in the twenty-first century. I sought the opinion of my cardiologist colleague, Dr. Roger Acheatel, who prescribed a series of diagnostic tests, including an echocardiogram and a stress test to evaluate cardiac function. While I did well on the stress test (I love stress), I failed the echocardiogram. Dr. Acheatel asked if I had a viral-like infection recently. I incorrectly said I had not. He said I had a pericardial effusion (excessive fluid around the heart). "You can see that in a patient with a postviral syndrome," he said.

About ten days later, I returned to the hospital for a repeat echocardiogram and hoping for a recovery. At that time, I confessed I'd had a viral-like illness in the month before the trip to Maui, but I just did not recall this fact when Dr. Acheatel took my history.

Echocardiogram results are immediately available when you are a personal friend of the cardiologist. Things had gotten worse. I now had a left pleural effusion (fluid accumulating in my left chest) with a resolving pericardial effusion. Acheatel said we need to tap that fluid and send it to the lab. That is another way of saying he was not certain what was going on, but it could be a postviral inflammatory process, it could be malignant, it could be infectious, or it could be some autoimmune-like disease. My dad never had any of this. Clearly, I am deviating from Mendel's law.

I went to the University of California, San Diego (UCSD), to see a cardiologist (second opinion) and a pulmonologist (also a second opinion). The cardiologist examined me and said, "There are no breath sounds in your left lower lobe." He clarified, "When I say 'no detectable breath sounds,' I mean 'second-year medical student nondetectable.'" Oops, more fluid in my left chest. It was now time for an interventional pulmonologist, Dr. George Cheng.

When a doctor has the word *interventional* in front of his or her specialty, that means he or she loves to perform invasive procedures—like going into your chest to look around. That was the plan when Dr. Cheng's nurse practitioner, who was learning to perform a pleural tap under his direction, asked me how I was doing. "Pretty well, considering you are about to stick a needle through my skin into my chest cavity," I said. "Please don't stick that needle into my lung; I need that organ to work as designed."

I had three pleural taps in four months. Each yielded a pint to a quart of fluid. What was happening to me? I consulted my research scientist, who was adept at internet searches, and found an article with a title like "Pericardial Effusion and Left Pleural Effusion: An Indicator of Coxsackie B Viral Infection." Wow, all this from the viral infection I'd had in January that I forgot to tell my cardiologist about.

I brought a copy of the peer-reviewed paper to the interventional pulmonologist, hoping that it presented a good argument for a noninvasive approach to my medical condition. I got sort of a shrug of the shoulders. It was clear I needed more proof.

As a pathologist, ordering laboratory tests is my specialty. I got to work and ordered all types of Coxsackie viral titers—that is, tests that could prove I had a Coxsackie viral infection recently. But before the results came back, I was talked into a thoracoscopy.

Thoracoscopy is a procedure in which your chest is penetrated by a narrow tube with a camera, and a biopsy tool is used to take portions of tissue from the chest wall. The principal risk is infection and a pneumothorax, a potentially fatal condition in which air collects in the space between your lungs and your chest wall and prevents the lung from expanding. I subjected myself to this risk because the results of my Coxsackie viral test were still pending—not an example of excellent decision-making.

The results came back positive. I had a Coxsackie viral infection, a virus known to cause myocarditis (inflammation of the heart muscle), tachycardia, arrhythmia (abnormal heart rhythm), and a general feeling of "What's happening to me?"

It is important to know that I had no symptoms during the few months of visiting the pulmonologist. In fact, when the pulmonologist asked how I was doing, I would always say that I felt great for twenty-nine or thirty days every month. "The only day I feel lousy is when I see you," I told him. "You tell me I am sick and that I need an interventional procedure." He smiled. I didn't.

Since I have worked in an acute-care hospital for over forty years, I know a lot of doctors. So I asked the opinion of the best pulmonologist I know. I told him the interventionalist was planning on performing a pleurodesis. That is a medical procedure in which the pleural space is artificially obliterated. Dr. Gregory Hirsch, the Palomar Medical Center pulmonologist (also an interventionalist), told me that pleurodesis is the only procedure pulmonologists perform that is extremely painful. And it works about 60 percent of the time.

What would I do? What was happening to me? Dr. Hirsch said that Coxsackie viral infections associated with pleural and pericardial effusions usually resolve on their own. Resolution occurs in a week or two, but sometimes it takes six months or more. The peer-reviewed case study I mentioned noted that the patient recovered six months after the diagnosis. Well, maybe I should do nothing!

Dr. Hirsch went over with me the rules taught to freshman medical students. The first rule is *primum non nocere*. This is Latin for "First, do no harm." I knew that, but what was I supposed to do? Then Hirsch said something that I had not heard before: "Jerry, you cannot make an asymptomatic patient feel better." That immediately made me feel better, and I did nothing.

On September 9, 2020, I strayed from my plan to avoid another chest X-ray and had one taken at UCSD. No pleural effusion detected! "Doing nothing" worked perfectly, and right on time. My conclusion is the virus read the same paper I did. It knew it had six months of mischief. Then the neutralizing antibodies would end this. And that is just what happened.

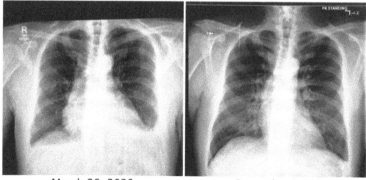

| March 26, 2020 | September 9, 2020 |

I waited and won. My chest X-ray on the right shows resolution of the pleural effusion visible in the X-ray on the left. That's a good thing.

Dr. Gregory Hirsch.

Dr. Roger Acheatel.

THIRTEEN

Retirement

On Retirement

At the age of seventy-two, I held two full-time jobs. One was president of the company I had founded in 1991, Valley Pathology Medical Associates Inc., and medical director of the Palomar Health Laboratories. The second and more time-consuming was chief quality officer (CQO) reporting to the CEO. I had been working in the quality office since 2005, when the CEO at that time, Michael Covert, asked me to join him in his efforts to achieve a high-reliability organization. In other words, Michael said, "Let's see if you can do something with all those degrees you have." It was an exciting time—the most challenging of my forty-two-year career.

But the excitement came to an abrupt ending. Officially, I was laid off on January 4, 2019, but I had known it was coming for a couple of months. Even more surprising was my response to the news of the elimination of my position. When the CEO told me of her reorganization, instead of challenging or even discussing the issue, I asked if I got severance pay. "Absolutely," she said.

I was delighted and saddened at the same time. This was the end of a chapter. But the severance pay was financially equivalent to retiring at seventy-three. Actuarially and considering family history, death at eighty-four to eighty-six was reasonable and perhaps likely. So at seventy-two, I figured I had about fourteen years left. Given the choice, should I be pushing myself to address 7:00 a.m. meetings and workdays that conclude at 8:00 p.m. or later? If I had a choice, I probably would have said, "I love work, and right now it feels good, so let's roll the dice for another year as CQO."

Of course, I didn't have that choice. It was over. But now I go to sleep without setting an alarm. With a few exceptions, I can arrive at work in the pathology lab at 9:00 a.m. or later if I desire. I enjoy going to bed and getting up when I feel like it. To me, that is the definition of decadence. And it happened only because Palomar Health changed its organizational structure. I am loving this, but I would not have known how much fun this could be without being shoved out—with a small fortune! Was this a blessing in disguise?

I am trying to understand my next chapter. I've turned the page of the book, but the next page is blank. A close friend and fellow resident in pathology at the National Institutes of Health, Michael Orlando, gave me an assignment to read "Of Solitude" by Michel de Montaigne. "Socrates says that the young should get instruction; that grown men should practice doing good; and that old men"—me—"should withdraw from all civil and military occupations and live at their own discretion, without being tied down to any fixed office," Montaigne wrote. Is it hedonistic to live life at one's own discretion?

To help me adjust, I visited the self-help section of the library and found *How to Live, or A Life of Montaigne in One Question and Twenty Attempts at an Answer* by Sarah Bakewell. I read the book. After considering Montaigne's advice to "old men," I realize my life has always been lived at my own discretion. I've been retired for decades. I just didn't know it.

Epilogue

Why did I write this book? Writing is a form of therapy for a guy who loves work. A quotation from *The Prophet* by Kahlil Gibran comes to mind: "Work is love made visible." In his chapter "On Work," the philosopher says, "Always you have been told that work is a curse and labour a misfortune. But I say to you that when you work you fulfill a part of the earth's furthest dream, assigned to you when that dream was born, and in keeping yourself with labour you are in truth loving life, and to love life through labour is to be intimate with life's inmost secret."*

Sometimes spontaneous thoughts take me to life's innermost secrets. Other times I need a catalyst to enter the sanctum. These essays are my key to the sacred place and shift me from thoughts to feelings. Some would say that once you've ascended from thoughts to feelings, you have reached the highest level of knowledge. That's where I like to be.

When in the act of writing, I become intimate with life, as evidenced by the tears of happiness that welled in my eyes describing a memory, as in the essay called "Pineapple Upside-Down Cake." Other times it was heartwarming to acknowledge the value of giving as in "Sweet Stories" and "The Thank-You Card." Just the thought of "The Hemoglobin Is Significantly Elevated" reliably generates a smile and often a laugh.

For me, writing amplifies happiness and quells the bitterness and anger we all experience through the years. Why did I write this book? At first, it was for me. Now I hope my stories will open a sacred place in the reader, permitting connection to the highest level of knowledge—feeling.

* Kahlil Gibran, *The Prophet* (New York: Knopf, 1995).

Acknowledgments

D r. James Stanley, a noted pediatric cardiovascular surgeon at the University of Michigan, wrote two books on his life. I read them both. Then I shared with him some of my essays on Michigan. He suggested that I compile and publish them. Then he said something that surprised me. He said I needed an editor.

I thought Microsoft Word replaced editors with its spelling and grammar functions. Jim said you couldn't proceed without an editor who understands you and is willing to work with you without changing your voice.

I found John Cannon, a retired editor for the *San Diego Union-Tribune*, who was nominated for a Pulitzer Prize for his work. Talented individuals who achieve greatness do not just take on assignments because of financial incentives. John said I should send him a few of my essays, and he would tell me if we could work together.

Of course, I sent John a half dozen essays and wondered if they were worthy of the time commitment from a Pulitzer Prize nominee. When he said he would take the job, I felt like I won the Nobel Prize in literature.

I really found a teacher. John listened and taught me about style and logical thought progression when communicating in writing. Microsoft Word cannot do that.

This book was made possible by John Cannon. I am no longer sure I understand the difference between an author and an editor. John said we are part of a team. He said, "Think Michigan football. You have a lot of players, but you need a head coach." I'm not sure if that is him or me.

Books

Movies

Music

Index

Page numbers in *italics* refer to photographs.

CPSIA information can be obtained
at www.ICGtesting.com
Printed in the USA
LVHW021741031021
699383LV00006B/49/J